THE CHALLENGE
OF CHANGE

THE CHALLENGE OF CHANGE

THE ANGLICAN COMMUNION IN THE POST-MODERN ERA

MARK HARRIS

 CHURCH

Church Publishing Incorporated, New York

Library of Congress Cataloging-in-Publication Data

Harris, Mark, 1940–
  The challenge of change : the Anglican Communion in the
  post-modern era / by Mark Harris.

  Includes bibliographical references.
  ISBN 0-89869-277-6 (pbk.)
  1. Anglican Communion.   I. Title.
BX5005.H34   1998   98-11460
283—dc21   CIP

Church Publishing Incorporated
445 Fifth Avenue
New York, NY 10016

5 4 3 2 1

To Kathryn,
whose open heart is a garden,
within which there is room for the whole world,
and thus for me.

CONTENTS

ACKNOWLEDGMENTS viii

INTRODUCTION 1

CHAPTER ONE 23
FINDING THE ANGLICAN COMMUNION

CHAPTER TWO 67
AN ANGLICAN COMMUNION UNDERSTANDING OF THE CHURCH
A Community of Mutuality

CHAPTER THREE 90
THEOLOGY ROOTED IN THE INCARNATION

CHAPTER FOUR 124
ENGAGEMENT WITH THE WORLD
The Practice of Incarnational Living

CHAPTER FIVE 158
VOCATIONAL RECOMMENDATIONS FOR THE ANGLICAN COMMUNION

BIBLIOGRAPHY 182

ABOUT THE AUTHOR 187

ACKNOWLEDGEMENTS

The opportunity to work on this book came about because a number of people provided encouragement and support. Kathryn and Matthew Harris have over and over again supported my dreams and visions. Bill Wood heard my doubts and hopes and accepted them both. Ian Douglas, Fredrica Harris Thompsett and many others at the Episcopal Divinity School challenged me to dig deeper, write better, and think more clearly about these matters. Ed and Gladys Rodman adopted me and sent me off to school in the morning, and heard my reports when I came in at night. The people of St. James' Millcreek Hundred took me on as rector while I was in the middle of my studies and gave me time to complete this work. It was quite generous of them for, after all, what they really wanted was a rector. Colleagues at the Episcopal Church Center, particularly those in the various offices concerned with World Mission, were a major support and encouragement for my education while I was on the staff with them. And here at the end of this particular process I have had even further encouragement from Frank Tedeschi, managing editor of Church Publishing Incorporated. These are blessings. What is good in this book grew from the goodness of these and many others. What is not so good is clearly my own doing.

INTRODUCTION

At the checkout counter he was asked if he could provide some identification. He looked intently at his image reflected in the store window, pointed, and said, "Yes, it's me, all right." The clerk was not amused. "Listen buddy, who you think you are is no business of mine. You could be anybody. What I want is proof."

Anglicans mostly define themselves by reflecting on their experience, by a process of self-authentication rather than external or independent definition.[1] While every group and individual self-definition is in some way formed by experience, we look for an identity whose character transcends the experience of who we are. We look for proof of our identity in a reason for being, beyond the fact of being. Most Anglicans feel that their reason for being is bound up not with being Anglicans but with being *Christians*. That is, our purpose for being is bound up with the call to new life in Jesus Christ. *Our experience* is in living out that purpose as Anglicans.

Some who call themselves Anglicans will not agree with generalizations of this sort, but that is true of virtually any statement made about Anglicans. Yet it seems clear to me that what distinguishes us as Anglicans from other Christians is precisely our experience of the peculiar fellowship found in our worship, and our identification through it with the ancient faith of the universal church. At times it has been a source of frustration to members of other religious communities to find Anglicans unwilling to define themselves more carefully in terms of a distinct theology or doctrine, with a separate and defined purpose. Some of our own better thinkers have felt the same way. Still, John Howe, first Secretary General of the Anglican Consultative Council, has clearly and forcefully argued against seeking a rigorous sense of self: "Anglicans think in terms of one continuing and universal Church. There is no separate Anglican identity. To search for one, as some ecumenists feel they must, is an unprofitable exercise."[2]

Anglicans have a continuity of experience in common prayer and sacrament that makes for a sense of community. There are now some seventy-five million persons around the globe who draw on the prior experience of the people of England at prayer. We are "in communion" with one another, sharing an understanding of sacrament and ministry. We have adopted what we have received and modified it to fit new situations. We are diverse enough now that various of us have drawn on our inheritance of prayer and sacrament in different ways, but there is the sense that our experience still calls us to fellowship with one another in ways that feel familiar—like family. This family of churches, or as it is sometimes described, "this fellowship," is what we have come to call the Anglican Communion. The experience of this fellowship is what casts the widest net for what we mean by being Anglican. Yet this fellowship is also elusive, for it rests, like the notion of Anglicanism itself, on no distinctive theological or doctrinal base. Anglicans do not believe in the Anglican Communion, they experience it. What we *believe* is both more ancient and universal.

Why then the Anglican Communion? Why Anglicans? On what do we justify this fellowship? From the standpoint of faith, rather than historical or sociological analysis, I suggest two possible responses.

The first stresses God's actions in history. The Anglican Communion is our experience because God the Holy Spirit has given it to us as a heritage from which we draw sustenance and strength, and from which we develop into greater maturity as people of God. We look to our history for a sense of the unfolding of God's will for us. In this sense, the Anglican Communion is a gift of the Holy Spirit. It is not necessarily the gift for many Christians, nor is it perhaps a greater gift, but it is ours. Lest this be thought a triumphalist statement, remember that it is often the most difficult gifts, those that may not even seem like gifts, but more like burdens, that mold and form us into what God really wants us to be.

The second response stresses the notion of instrumentality. The Anglican Communion is justified only as an instrument of God's will for God's purpose. Here we look at our fellowship experience not as a gift, but rather as a means to an end known only to the Holy Spirit. In this sense, the communion is one of many ways by which the Holy Spirit heals and restores. If this is so, we find our answer in the future, where it will become clear just what purpose we serve. But we know at least that our purpose lies not in who we believe we are, but in what God is doing with us.

The two responses coalesce. The Anglican Communion is a gift that we experience fully, if sometimes with difficulty; and it serves God's purposes, which we do not know fully by experience but only by faith. The Anglican Communion is not something in which we believe; rather, it is experienced. Our experience as Anglicans contributes to our belief in the fulfillment of God's will for all of creation. Our experience as Anglicans is the place where we begin, and the place where we are led is the fulfillment of the mission of the church, which is to "restore all people to unity with God and each other in Christ."[3]

I am assuming that the Anglican Communion is a *reality* experienced often enough by enough people that it makes sense to ask just what grows from that experience. In this book I want to explore the commitments we have with one another now and what might they look like in the future. As Anglicans, we know that this companionship entails the willingness to break bread together, to share *communion*. But it means, too, a willingness to share thoughts and words and dreams about God, about life and death, resurrection and service. For if we are on the Way and on pilgrimage, and being Anglican is our experience of that walk, there will be time to talk. What are our commitments to one another such that we are willing to continue in these conversations as we walk together?

THE EXPERIENCE OF THE ANGLICAN COMMUNION

Eridard and Jane are Ugandans and Christians, she a nurse and he a priest of the (Anglican) Church of (the Province of) Uganda.[4] I met them in December 1987 in Mityana, Uganda, on a Sunday afternoon. I had just recently been appointed the Coordinator of Overseas Personnel for the Episcopal Church and was visiting the Diocese of Mityana as part of an orientation to the work of the church in East Africa. I must admit I was a little prideful about being the personnel officer of a sizable missionary "sending" organization, and was basking in the still warm glow of this new position. I was also tired from meetings I had just attended, ones filled with abstractions about mission service and the church.

The Bishop had asked if I would like to come to a small party at the cathedral for a couple going as missionaries from the Diocese of Mityana to a diocese in Zimbabwe in the Church of the Province of Central Africa. These were the first missionaries being sent from the diocese, he said, and they were very happy to be finally sending some of their own into mission beyond their church.

The cathedral sat out in the open countryside. We gathered in one of the classroom buildings. I remember the cool interior of the room where the party was, and the smell of tea brewing. It was there I first met Eridard and Jane. There was delight and laughter, and good words and feelings for these two. They were being sent on their way rejoicing, just as missionaries should always been sent. I remember, too, that it was all very new for them. I understood that there, in that country cathedral in Uganda, I was witness to the beginning of a new work in Jesus Christ, a new connection between peoples of faith, a new ministry in the making. Meeting Eridard and Jane put quite a lot in perspective, both humbling my pride and lifting my spirits at a time when I needed both.

That experience was for me a confirmation that the Anglican Communion is *real* and that what at times seems the most ethereal of conceptualizations is as concrete as any union between or among people. Eridard and Jane were being sent from one community to another as a sign of the care and love we experience in Jesus Christ. That sending and receiving was taking place in communities that understood the practical effects of mutuality, of communion, of fellowship. They were sent from one place to another within the same larger community, in which sacraments and word are shared. Eridard and Jane are participants in the wider fellowship of Anglican churches. And that fellowship is real.

There are other times, of course, when the communion has seemed to be a very thin and wispy reality. A good friend, Fred Howard, once returning tired from a meeting about an Anglican Communion electronic network, told me that he sometimes wondered if there *was* any such thing as the Anglican Communion. He was fairly sure he had not seen or experienced it on that trip! Sometimes the notion of the Anglican Communion seems a shadow, not a reality at all.

Indeed, there are times when the notion of the communion seems irrelevant, particularly when held up against the local experience of church. Our life in the church, in its immediate and experienced sense, in prayer and action locally, is often profoundly relevant. Church fellowship has its deepest meaning when it refers to the particular community and place where at one time or another we may briefly meet God. Fred and Eridard and Jane, each Presiding Bishop, even the Archbishop of Canterbury and we, are all members of such communities of faith. These are always local, always grounded in the work of prayer, thanksgiving, and witness that marks us as *Christian*, rather than as Episcopalian or Anglican. Given the base-reality of our Christian faith, our awareness of our Anglicanism sometimes seems a secondary consideration and not worthy of our time. But it does draw our attention when it is experienced as opening into a greater sharing of life in the Body of Christ.

The phrase "the Anglican Communion" is really a shorthand device for talking about a particular commitment among various churches and peoples as *companions on the Way of Christ*. It was a phrase coined in the mid-nineteenth century to describe the relationship that was desired, and realized in some instances, among the churches that traced their sources and understanding of word, creed, sacrament, and historic episcopate by way of the Church of England. It may first have been used in 1851, in the conversations calling for a conference of all bishops whose orders derived from, and who were in communion with, the See of Canterbury.[5] The first of these meetings was held in 1867, and there the term "Anglican Communion" was used regularly. These conferences came to be called the Lambeth Conferences. They have been held every ten years except during wartime.

These bishops who gather are jurisdictional ministers—that is, they usually focus the ministries of a group of parishes with their clergy and people, in a given geographical region, called a diocese. Thus, the communion is usually envisioned as a fellowship not only of bishops but of their dioceses. The primary practical links among the bishops and dioceses have been prayer, missionary engagement, and gatherings for communion-based fellowship. The most significant sign of these links is the Lambeth Conference. Quite recently, four "instruments of unity" have been suggested as ways of linking the communion. They are (1) the Archbishop of Canterbury, (2) the Lambeth Conference, (3) the Primates' Meeting and (4) the Anglican Consultative Council.[6]

The commitment to companionship on the Way is evolving, even as this book is being written, but I would maintain that the basic reason for talking about the communion has not changed. We talk about the Anglican Communion because we are members not only of our local church and of a diocesan community but are also linked *by affection* to people all over the world who share the commitment to a common understanding of life in Christ. Our bishops may be the primary focus of that connection, but the thread that connects appears in many forms: in Eridard and Jane going from Uganda to Zimbabwe; in a companion diocese relationship; in prayers on Sunday from the *Anglican Cycle of Prayer*; in the visit by someone from another part of the communion to our parish because it is Sunday and they were looking for an Anglican church in which to worship. It exists, too, when we pray and worry for a political prisoner like Terry Waite, or when we give for the work of the church in Jerusalem or for relief for the people of Rwanda or Haiti. As with most realities of human relationship, the Anglican Communion must be *experienced* if it is to be taken seriously.

The Vocation of the Anglican Communion

This book assumes that the Anglican Communion is a reality. It also assumes that the Anglican Communion has a vocation. It is has a purpose that lies beyond it and which can be known only by envisioning it. This book is an attempt to explore a vision: a vision of the vocation of the Anglican Communion for the near future.

I use the word *vision* in part because we often use it to talk about finding our way to a new understanding. We ask, "What is your vision of the future of this organization?" Or, "What vision do you have of our role as a church?" But I also want to use the word in the religious sense. The hope to develop an understanding of the vocation of the Anglican Communion is not finally something in which vision is a planning tool alone, but in which vision is an immediate grasp of the whole. That is, *vision* here means both a process of envisioning and an immediate "seeing."

My involvement with this process and "seeing" is a consequence of twelve years on the Presiding Bishop's staff, working on behalf of the Episcopal Church in its relation to other provinces of the Anglican Communion; of missionary experience in Puerto Rico; and of years of "domestic" missionary work in campus ministry. In reflecting on the experiences of others and on my own experience, I have envisioned the Anglican Communion in various ways.

Sometimes the communion has seemed an almost physical presence, as when Archbishop Desmond Tutu addressed a student conference in the U.S., or when students from many different countries met at a seminar table at the College of the Ascension in England, or when the Archbishop of Canterbury stood in the Cathedral in Seoul to give over jurisdiction of the Anglican Church of Korea to that new province.

At other times, the communion has seemed less a presence and more a specter, lurking about in the shadows of churches still unable to move beyond a sense of being outcroppings of proper English religion in strange surroundings. Sometimes I imagine the Anglican Communion as a corporation, sometimes as an aid society. Some images call up potentates and curias, others table fellowship and mutuality.

So it seems to me that some effort is needed to sort out those images and to consider which has a claim on us. I believe that in sorting out these images we can have a vision of what the communion could be. This vision makes a claim on my allegiance. These pages describe the envisioning process, and hopefully the immediate seeing. I hope the reader will also be moved by something of the same process and vision.

At the same time I am loath to suggest that anyone have a vision of anything for the "new millennium." The years that mark the end of a century and the beginning of a new one are filled with the same dung and glory as all other years. To mark them out specially as turning points is arbitrary and somewhat idolatrous. Any reason for this envisioning at this particular time is related to the much larger concerns that face all Christians as we encounter and are challenged by postmodernist thought. Still reeling from the struggle to live with the secularization of the objective sciences, the church must now learn to live with a more and more fluid and complex interweaving of ideas, themes, and intellectual constructs that constitute the post-modern period. Vision and vocation are needed if this church, and in fact the whole church, is to come to grips with the profound changes now occurring.

Having a vision of the future of the communion is not at all like having that vision come true. The Anglican Communion might develop in the future in ways that I would find difficult to accept. I do not believe, for example, that the world needs more patriarchs, authoritarian promulgators of doctrine, or narrow religious separatists; and should we develop in such a way, I would be greatly saddened. Further, I am convinced that the irrelevance of international religious organizations is directly proportional to these organizations' attempts to direct rather than serve, to support purity codes rather than compassionate action. An Anglican Communion that became an instrument of corporate control would serve our heritage, and us, poorly. The Anglican Communion could indeed become something I would consider either abhorrent or irrelevant.

Everyone who attempts to envision a positive future does so on the basis of prior commitments. My rejection of some futures for the communion and my embracing of others grows from an already informed conscience. I contend that, as Anglicans, we are predisposed to want certain sorts of futures and to reject others. However, that predisposition only holds when we remember who we are. For this reason a good bit of this book will be a reminder of what we do have as an Anglican inheritance.

It seems to me also that church is best formed "from the bottom up," and even its grandest schemes for doctrinal exactness or ritual purity must finally give way to the prophetic centrality of the community that gathers. That community is always local.[7] At the same time, even with the bottom-up sensibility, many of us very much love the peculiar larger church called the Episcopal Church, and we highly value its being collected with other Anglican churches in prayer and common life. We have every intention of contributing what we can to make life together, as churches in communion, a source of service to the world, reflecting the openness that is possible in a compassionate community. The predisposition to do so is itself a product of our attending to the church we love and of its unfolding role in the Body of Christ.

What I want to explore might first be put as a question: What form *should* the Anglican Communion take in the next years? Clearly I am not asking what form we *can expect* the communion to take, as based on what it is now or has been in the past. Nor am I suggesting that there is any clear sense of what the Anglican Communion is now, so that the future would need either to remedy defects in, or to codify, the communion's current form. In a sense, my question is purely visionary. It does not begin as a predictive or normative question. It is an admittedly peculiar question, as are all envisioning questions; so it helps to get a sense of what I would count as responses. Here are some examples of such answers.

(1) *The Anglican Communion should become a reasonably coherent worldwide church,* with many regional parts often, but not exclusively, consisting of national churches. It should have a well-defined theology and polity, so that it can enter, as a world body, into discussions of unity and the reunion of Christian churches. It should have a strong internal sense of unity and authority and bring that to the table with other communions where the ecumenical future of Christianity is discussed. It should have a clear structure of authority, so that its leaders are empowered to speak *for* the Anglican Communion.

(2) *The Anglican Communion should be understood as a product of the fellowship of the Lambeth Conference,* where bishops are literally in

communion with the Archbishop of Canterbury. That is, it should be understood as a particular case of the sharing of the sacred meal and table fellowship, something that Christians experience in a variety of settings. This particular experience of *koinonia* would be shared by very few. It would extend from the bishops in community at Lambeth to certain other international gatherings of church people, as well as to visits among provinces, and it would be echoed in prayers for member dioceses of the communion. But that is all: it would only be seen as existing for the users, who are mostly influential and fortunate enough to have such experiences. For most members of the churches whose bishops meet at Lambeth, the Anglican Communion would be pictures of those people meeting, pictures of the Archbishop of Canterbury or symbols like the Compass Rose emblem of the communion, prayers said at the intercessions, or the pamphlet descriptions of organizations that provide aid to those in need across the communion. In this sense, for most of us, the communion would be known only in an iconographic way, by signs and symbols.

(3) *The Anglican Communion should be understood as an intellectual construct, based on the reality of the local congregation.* That is, it should not be taken as the reality of the church, but only reflect it. Reality would lie in the local congregation, linked in mutual respect and canon by bishops. In this vision, the provincial system of national churches would develop and depend on the collegial will of diocesan bishops and dioceses. The real center of the Anglican churches would be in the diocese. As a construct, the Anglican Communion would be valuable because it would affirm interconnectedness among the Anglican churches and would support local dioceses in their struggles to be the Body of Christ. Ultimately, the realities of authority and identity would dictate that all authoritative links would be within provincial structures. One or another of the Anglican provinces would feel free to proceed with actions others might not agree with. The communion would be an idea without directive or coercive power, or even sometimes much influence.

(4) *The Anglican Communion should be "a fellowship within the One, Holy, Catholic and Apostolic Church."* We should view the communion as a community, a part—and only a part—of the church

universal. As a *koinonia,* a community of mutuality, it would have every voluntary reason for being together in communion and every historic reason for gathering at conferences chaired by the Archbishop of Canterbury. But the primary commitment to this fellowship would be as an instrument for unity and mutuality. That unity would call us beyond the limits of Anglican fellowship, and our mutuality would call us away from doctrinal or political peculiarity. Its only distinctive "doctrines," which it should hold in trust for the future of the church, would be the call to be comprehensive and the belief that all theology is provisional.

The reader deserves to know just where I stand; of these responses to the question of form, I will argue that the fourth is most appropriate. *The Anglican Communion should be supported and encouraged as a fellowship, a* koinonia, *rather than as an organization per se.* And we should support a vision of the communion in which its vocation is to model through fellowship an attempt at comprehensiveness in the Body of Christ.

Of course, on some level all these visions are appropriate. The Anglican Communion is a worldwide church, a product of the Lambeth Conference, an intellectual construct, and a "fellowship." But the question is whether churches that call themselves Anglican throughout the world are drawn more to one or the other of these models, and whether our vision of the Anglican Communion *should* come to resemble one or another of these descriptions.

WHY THE QUESTION OF VISION NOW?
THE CHALLENGE TO FIND AN IDEOLOGY

There is a particular reason for asking this question in these days. The pressure is on, within the Episcopal Church and to some extent among the various churches of the Anglican Communion, to describe the boundaries within which Anglicans can claim a sense of special calling, purpose, and reason for being. That is, there is a call for an Anglican *ideology.*[8] This call is often stated as the desire to describe the limits of inclusion, so that people can reach some consensus on moral, ecclesial and social issues. The question gets asked, "Is there a basis in Anglican thought and life for specific moral, theological, and social teachings? And if so, what effect does this have on the way we view ourselves and our mutuality throughout the communion?"

For Anglicans, the problem that most strikingly brought matters to a head was that of the ordination of women in some, but not all, of the provinces. The lack of a unified response was disturbing to those who looked for coherence in the communion. The center (however defined) seemed not to be holding. And if it did not hold on that issue, how much moreso might it not hold on other moral and theological issues?

In this time of theological disunity, the Inter-Anglican Theological and Doctrinal Commission was established as a context in which to begin to sort out the matter of how we might continue to hold things together theologically. The commission has devoted much effort to trying to understand what it means to be Anglican.[9] It is only partly succeeding.

Certainly there are many variations in the way Anglicans respond to theological and moral issues, both in particular churches and throughout the communion. The responses all resound with clashing claims of authority: canons require, justice demands, or tradition supports; God has a preference for the poor, the law-abiding, the wise, or the foolish; scripture supports, rejects, or is silent on a variety of matters; and so on. These variations in Anglican thought raise questions of identity and authority. Some would suggest that Anglicans have a special problem with identity and press strongly for a new means of deciding just who we are.

THE BREAKDOWN OF MODERNITY AND CHRISTENDOM

My sense, however, is that these questions are not about Anglican identity or Anglican authority per se. We have no particular corner on the market of religious confusion about identity and authority. There is much to suggest that these questions are mostly about (1) our growing doubts about the intellectual paradigm of the Enlightenment and (2) being Christians in post- or extra- Christian societies. That is, our confusions are to a large extent about what has become known as *modernity*.

Western European thought has been caught up in the full flower of modernity, and to some extent so has the whole world. Modernity is a notably successful product of the Enlightenment paradigm and has contributed greatly to the blossoming of scientific thought. That paradigm suggests, among other things, a split between the external and internal worlds, such that objective sciences could be developed and subjective processes understood. Our mental furniture has been thoroughly arranged with the basic distinction between objective and subjective environments in mind. The objective environments were those in which sciences could be developed. Some areas that seemed subjective have since come to be seen as objective, as mental processes have come to be more clearly understood as physiological functions. Scientific thinking has come to view social constructs (organizations, corporations, etc.) as objects to be analyzed, taken apart and put back together again, and fixed. Subjective environments have been understood as places where ideologies could be developed in response to the need for order. Moral and theological questions have often been understood as subjective and ideological.

While the reasons are too complex to be easily stated here, it would seem that in this century there has been a breakdown of many elements of the Enlightenment paradigm.[10] The distinction between objective sciences and subjective ideologies has not been satisfactorily maintained. The scandal of modernity is that it has produced both ideologically deformed scientific thinking and scientifically enhanced ideologies. Modernity has given us megalomaniacs with the tools to sway millions and the bombs to destroy them.

The result of this breakdown is a greater dissonance between the search for truth and the ability to grasp it. The effects of the shift in paradigm away from Enlightenment thought are still unclear; but we do know that the shift includes a move from thought processes that are linear, logical, and organizational to ones that resemble networks, matrices, and organisms.

Over a much longer time the church has seen one of its own paradigms gradually destroyed. The church as experienced first in the Roman Empire, and then in the larger western culture, worked within a paradigm where church and state were mutually accountable to one another as instruments of God's grace and justice. The church provided the moral and theological context in which the state would exercise power and authority. The works of the two systems, church and state, were seen as totally integrated. This is often called the paradigm of Christendom.

The breakdown of this paradigm occurred as the Holy Roman Empire devolved into city- and nation-states and as these, in turn, were confronted with the "free thinking" of the Enlightenment and the pluralism of an ever-widening world view. Without a cohesive empire, and with no objective truth to religious claims, Christendom's relationship between church and society could no longer hold. The church would no longer have the authority to teach and compel, and the state would no longer see itself as an agent for God's justice. Signs of the breakdown of this paradigm continue in the present.

As the paradigms of modernity are being challenged, it is fascinating to see churches using the paradigms of objective social sciences in an attempt to repair themselves. While it is sometimes useful to fix an objective "thing" (i.e., the church as organization), that effort completely misses the challenge presented by the emergence of post-modern paradigms. If the church is not an object that can be "fixed," but an organism that is growing and changing and has a life, then the paradigms for understanding it are quite different. For example, instead of thinking primarily about organizing *to do,* we might begin thinking more often about *being*—seeing ourselves as an organism whose value is determined not by product, but by presence.

The paradigm of Christendom is collapsing, and we are not sure just what will replace it. Just as we live in a "post-modern" world, we also live now in a "post-Christian" world. That is, just as the paradigm of modernity is increasingly unsatisfactory, so too, the paradigm of Christendom. This makes it more difficult to maintian the way church beliefs are developed, taught, and accepted.

For all Christians who value an understandable faith, this is a time of tentativeness, of "feeling our way." Authority and identity are questions we face, not as a special Anglican problem, but as part of the general situation of church people whose thinking has been formed by paradigms of Christendom and modernity and who now see their limitations. Yet it is humbling to realize that more and more of those we meet as fellow Anglicans in other parts of the world do not share these paradigmatic problems, or at least do not share them to the same extent. Some of them see the issue of Anglican authority or identity as a peculiar problem of Anglo-Saxon Christianity and specifically "northern" or "western."

In discussions among "western" or "northern" Christians this is also a time when all sorts of solutions to modernity's limitations are proposed, most of which recall previous solutions to the issues of identity and authority. Many American Christians seem quite willing to blame modernity for their current confusion and look longingly to a past golden period of intellectual and theological stability. I note, however, that very few of these Christians suggest that we throw out the benefits of modernity as well as its limitations. Looking backwards does not extend to doing without anesthesia, telephones, or indoor plumbing.

There are many Christians who are disturbed by the suggestion that we should live for a while with provisional responses or with a comprehensive sensibility allowing the theologically opposed to eat at the same table. We seem to be in a time when the force of confessionally defined, exclusive Christianity is on the rise. The shrill cry of "heresy!" is heard more often and is raised against those who look beyond the edges of the paradigms of Christendom and modernity.

Those of us who believe that we are called *beyond* modernity, rather than back to some pre-modern structures of thought and belief, must ask if there is an Anglican sensibility that would allow a provisional and comprehensive way forward when so many, including some Anglicans, are calling for a definitive and exclusive religious response. And if so, are Anglicans motivated to express that sensibility?

AN ANGLICAN VOCATION

The concern of Anglicans to find right responses to the issues of our time is similar to that of every community filled with the expectation that what is necessary for our well being can be known in nature or revealed in religion. The problems faced when scientific knowledge and religious revelation fail are not particularly Anglican. They are shared by all who have been guided first by Enlightenment thinking and now see the need to move on.

But because of our peculiar history and theological explorations, Anglicans may have a special vocational opportunity to model ways to live beyond the paradigms of the Enlightenment, to live with ambiguity at a time when the security of right answers is not available. I will argue that there is much to be hoped for in this regard, but only if we have the willingness to live in times of great ambiguity and with a modest sense of our own path as a Christian community.

This vision, even incompletely formed, suggests that Anglicanism has a vocation to *discernment*. Ours is a vocation to attend to God's unfolding desire for us. It is a call away from what we have thought being Anglican—or for that matter being Christian—was about. It is also a vocation to model comprehensiveness. Throughout Christian history, and indeed world history, there have been individuals called to a vocation of comprehensiveness. Why not a whole religious community?

As a member and a priest of one of the churches in the Anglican Communion, the Episcopal Church, I am painfully aware that this vision to comprehensiveness (however we define it) is not adequately incarnated at present in our church. After all, the Episcopal Church is now viewed by most people as a denomination, one of many in the United States. Viewed as a denomination, the Episcopal Church is patently *not* comprehensive. For that matter neither is any other church in its part of the world. There is, on a practical level, no single church community that can claim to be comprehensive in its reflection of the catholic or universal Christian body. At the same time, I believe that the Episcopal Church and other churches in the Anglican Communion intend themselves to be particular communities in the one church universal, providing a welcoming environment for those who are trying to be theologically responsible and comprehensive in a post-Christian and post-modern world.

It should also be noted that, while the Episcopal Church might be viewed as a denomination in the United States, the Anglican Communion is not the same thing raised to an international level. The Anglican Communion does not propose to be the way of naming the "real" church universal, or to be a "world" religion. And it does not yield that right to other worldwide Christian bodies. This worldwide fellowship of churches, this *koinonia*, is neither confessionally determinative nor authoritatively central to the existence of any of its members. It is, in short, not principally an *organization*, but an *organism*.

The vision of the vocation of the Anglican Communion is seen, sometimes clearly and sometimes dimly, in the activities of this fellowship and in each member church's efforts to maintain fellowship in the face of great differences among the churches. It is also seen in the desires of member churches to move beyond the scandal of division. As a result, we are also called to a peculiar sort of ecumenical agenda, one that grows from the need for openness among ourselves. We have become a bridge-building church community by internal necessity. Those bridges can be of value to the ecumenical community as well.

When we do try to describe ourselves as Anglicans, so that persons of other churches understand that we are speaking not only of our experience, but that of most other Anglicans, high on the list of ideals is that of comprehensiveness. But let us be clear here as well: the identification with comprehensiveness is not about the past, nor even about the present. It is about the future. It represents an *ideal* toward which we are moving, God willing, as we are able. It is about envisioning our vocation.

I will argue for the following as defining goals of the Anglican vocation for the next period of the communion's development:

(1) *In its structure, a community of mutuality.* Anglicanism understands itself not as *the* church, but as a fellowship within the one, holy, catholic and apostolic church. It proposes to structure its life within the whole church on the model of mutuality grounded in the idea of *koinonia*. It sees its structure as provisional. The *koinonia* in which its structure is grounded finds outward and visible expression in the sacramental life.

(2) *In its envisioning theology, incarnational.* Anglican theology is characterized by its willingness to be informed by scripture, tradition, and reason. Its method is pragmatic and comprehensive. The characteristic theology of Anglicanism is grounded in an emphasis on the doctrine of the incarnation. Like its structure, its doctrinal formulations are understood to be provisional.

(3) *In its engagement with the world, a compassionate communion.* Grounding its mission in the incarnation, the Anglican Communion seeks to embody the divine compassion which was made real in Jesus, and which continues to be experienced beyond all boundaries set by our own limitations.

WHY SELF-UNDERSTANDING CANNOT REPLACE VISION

Several Anglican theologians who have issued a call to tighten up Anglican self-understanding so that we can take our place as a separate world church are challenging this vision of a comprehensive and provisional fellowship. They argue that we need to do this in a Christendom divided so that we, too, can make the competitive case for our life as a world-class church.

Much recent thinking about the Anglican Communion has concerned its governance, that is, the question of authority in Anglicanism and how we exercise discipline on a communion-wide basis. The literature on this is surprisingly large, and the forces pushing for greater separate identity, clearer governance, and consistent discipline are formidable. Not surprisingly, this also leads to the temptation to establish or recommend new structures, new levels of authority, new ways to keep our separateness and distinctness intact. But where are we to find the sense of self-identity and understanding?

If this self-understanding is to arise from historical theology, then our own sinfulness as a church, particularly in missionary engagement, becomes definitive. Anglicanism took shape while the European powers, including England, were attempting world conquest. Several critics of our history are happy to point out that Anglicanism's adherents colluded in, or acquiesced to, the grab for land and power and kingdom-building. These factors contributed to the disparity of the distribution of wealth in Europe and reinforced the commerce in, and dependence on, slave labor. The self-giving of many missionaries is not at issue here, nor is their faithfulness. Whether or not the gospel of peace was spread by peaceful servants of God, the difficult fact remains that Anglicans mostly went where there was conquest to be had or business to be done by English-speaking peoples. The separation of the missionary church and the mercantile state was not at all clearly defined. If being Anglican is bound to a separate historical identity, then that identity is sin, and in particular the sins of greed and racism.

If, on the other hand, Anglican self-understanding is to be defined by engagement in a systematic or unified theology, our problem is somewhat different. For much of its history, Anglicanism has built on and amplified the Church of England's response to the problem of authority. Authoritative doctrine has been derived by reference to scripture, tradition, and reason, *in the context of the experience of the English people.* That experience has been expressed in the cooperative actions of state and church in an established religion. The remnants of the Constantinian church, that is the church of the Holy Roman Empire, are to be found in England in the state church and in the residual notion of prince bishops much in evidence even in the American church.

What this has meant in practice is that governance has borne equal weight with other sources in forming our theological self-understanding. This is clearly seen in the Lambeth Quadrilateral, where episcopal governance is put on the same level as scripture, sacraments, and creeds. This is really the only distinctive theological contribution that Anglicans (particularly English Anglicans) bring to the ecumenical discussion—we have given the issue of authority centrality and have spoken of a fellowship based on the notion of bishop and council, or on a different level, of primates and synods.[11]

If this is the theological identity of Anglicans—that we are *episcopal* churches—and if we define episcopacy as that "oversight" experienced by the English church, then our identity is bound again to sin, this time the sin of patriarchal and monarchical arrogance. In this context, to work for a more articulate and special Anglican theology is to work for a self-identity that alienates and belittles other peoples of faith who have no great love for or experience with monarchical bishops. Unless, as the Lambeth Quadrilateral suggests, there can be a wider sense of the episcopacy "locally adapted," the episcopate is a stumbling block, and therefore not conducive to comprehensive fellowship.

Thus, the problem with trying to develop a separate denominational theology, doctrine, or identity for Anglicans as a worldwide community is that our experience would seem to identify Anglicanism with the historical circumstances of a faith community that has spread its practices around the world in collusion with instruments of greed, racism, and monarchical arrogance.[12]

It is possible, I will argue, to disentangle ourselves from that collusion, but not if we try to justify a special vocation for Anglicanism on historical and theological grounds of peculiar experience. Our vocation lies not in the path that brought us here, but in the way we now walk and the places we are willing to go in following Jesus as Christ. We cannot discern the vocation of Anglicanism and the future of the Anglican Communion simply by knowing how we got where we are. Our definition lies in the future. The great deal of work that has been done in uncovering our history and theological concerns is useful, but only preliminary. Obviously, this vision, this call, is not now fully realized in Anglican communities. Our vocation, if accepted, will lead to the communion's own death, so that mutuality, incarnation, and compassion might abound.

In chapter 1 of what follows, I will briefly make some observations about how the Anglican Communion evolved in the context of modernity. In chapters 2–4 I will explore in greater depth the three elements of the vision for the Anglican Communion I have already named: the structure of a community of mutuality, an incarnational theology, and a mission of compassionate engagement. In the concluding chapter, I will summarize my recommendations for the vocation of the Anglican Communion in the coming years.

The premise of this work is that the Anglican Communion is an embodied entity and therefore has a life, that it has a vocation within that life, and that it will die. The issue then is not to be concerned with institutional immortality, but to be concerned with doing God's will. Self-identity will have its place, of course, but only insofar as that identity names us by our vocation. The vocation of the church, the Body of Christ, is one in which being Anglican is only a small part of the story, but it is a story worth the telling, and I hope worth the pondering.

ENDNOTES

1. The term *Anglican*, referring first to the Church of England (*Ecclesia Anglicana*) and later to certain churches formed outside the domain of the Church of England, began its modern use in the eighteenth and nineteenth centuries (see Sykes and Booty, *The Study of Anglicanism*, 406). I use the term *Anglican* here to describe a person or a church that is part of the Anglican Communion. For example, an Episcopalian is an Anglican, and the Episcopal Church is an Anglican church. Those churches that claim an Anglican heritage but are not in communion with the Archbishop of Canterbury are not here referred to as Anglican.

2. Howe, *Anglicanism & the Universal Church*, 28.

3. The Book of Common Prayer, 855.

4. Several problems of title and terminology need explanation here. The official name of the Anglican community in Uganda is simply "The Church of Uganda," but that name is singularly uninformative. The "Church of (the Province of) Uganda" is a bit more helpful, since *Province* (capitalized) is the normal designation of an autonomous church that is a member of the Anglican Communion. Many members of our own churches and our ecumenical friends still might not catch the fact that this is an Anglican designation, however; so in this text I will often add *(Anglican)* to make it clear that the church is a member of the Anglican Communion.

5. Avis, "What is 'Anglicanism'?" in Sykes and Booty, *The Study of Anglicanism*, 406–7.

6. Press release, "Eames: Lambeth 1998 the Most Defining in Our History" (Anglican Communion News Service: Oct. 14, 1996).

7. The locality can, of course, be anywhere, and it may last only for a short time. For instance, General Convention might be viewed as a local community lasting about two weeks; it might therefore make a prophetic utterance from its own experience. I believe it has in fact done so on occasion.

8. A preoccupation with issues of authority has brought wide attention to this call, but I believe it is too much centered on the Church of England. The ideological emphasis is most ably represented in the writings of Stephen Sykes.

9. The commission's "Virginia Report," presented to the Anglican Consultative Council in Panama in October 1996 (before the 1998 Lambeth Conference), is a primary work in progress.

10. David J. Bosch, "The Emergence of a Postmodern Paradigm," *Transforming Mission*, 349–62, provides a very brief but quite fine statement of the problem.

11. The "Virginia Report" of the Inter-Anglican Theological and Doctrinal Commission referred to such "instruments of unity," particularly the Primates' Meeting and the Anglican Consultative Council.

12. A picture of the Anglican Church (Church of England) as a mirror of the empire can be seen in the graphic and devastating comments of Mahatma Gandhi, whose writings on Christianity's presence in India are recorded in Ellsberg and Gandhi, *Gandhi on Christianity*.

CHAPTER 1

FINDING THE ANGLICAN COMMUNION

Francis Bacon (1561–1626) thought that three great inventions had ushered in the new world in which he lived—gunpowder, the mariner's compass and printing. Gunpowder contributed to the establishment of centralized national states in Europe, and to warfare between them; gunpowder and the mariner's compass between them made possible the extension of European domination and plunder over the whole world, and so to the enrichment of Europe. Printing extended knowledge.[1]

Francis Bacon lived at the front edge of what we now call modernity. Modernity is the name given to the period of history that covers the last four hundred years, roughly from the beginning of the seventeenth century to the mid-twentieth century.[2] Nested in modernity is the Enlightenment, generally considered the product of the eighteenth century. Bacon's three world-changing devices—gunpowder, the first moveable type press (ca. 1450), and the marine compass—were all products of the late medieval period. Their origins were not European, or at least not exclusively so, but it was Europe's fortune and misfortune alike that these devices were perfected in design in Europe in the Renaissance and Reformation periods and made economically accessible to a whole variety of people, companies, and nations.

The years from 1450 to 1600 completely transformed western Europe. It looked for the first time across oceans to the west and south for its adventures, not only to land routes east. The technologies for exploration and colonialism were developed in this period. As importantly, it was a time when Europeans learned the beginning skills of revolution, mostly by practicing it among themselves.

It was a time when intellectual life expanded with a new freedom, fed by the information explosion of the printed word. It was a time of renaissance. It was a time when Christendom made its greatest effort to make *church* better. It was a time for reformation. It was also the time in which a distinctly English understanding of church began to be articulated. The origins of Anglicanism date from this period, just before what is called the Modern Age.[3]

"The Anglican Communion," as a name, was first used in about 1850. It is this period of about 250 years in which the guiding sensibilities of Anglicanism were articulated, preparations were made, and experiences were had, that led to the naming of a perceived worldwide collection of churches. Anglicanism was formed as the west was becoming the "modern world," and the Anglican Communion is a product of that world. It is no wonder, then, that as the paradigms and models based on the presuppositions of the west are now being challenged, the Anglican Communion might also find itself confronted by its own rootedness in modernity.

Historians are everywhere, and so are their analyses of the meaning of events and movements. There are very good histories available dealing with the Renaissance, the Reformation, the Enlightenment, the Church of England, and Anglicanism. It would do both these historians and the reader a disservice to try to say too much more about the rather complex weaving of issues and concerns during this period. But there are some historical notes that do seem appropriate to the topic of this book. I suggest we look at them in three areas: themes of Anglicanism; Anglicanism as experienced by its receivers; and Anglican Communion concerns in the late twentieth century.

Most studies of Anglicanism are written as if we were following a path through centuries of English history, paths which in the seventeenth to the nineteenth centuries would lead to the new world of churches that are Anglican but not in England. That is, the viewpoint is precisely *English*. But our concerns are about *the Anglican Communion*. A history of the whole Anglican Communion might better begin by recounting what it was like to have these English come and bring this religion with them. The Anglican Communion begins really with the first awareness that the religion which first appeared as English was now truly located in many places and was no longer merely English. I want briefly to make some observations about the history of the Anglican Communion viewed from *outside the English Church*. These will, I hope, prepare the groundwork for examining some contemporary issues regarding the communion as a whole.

THEMES OF ANGLICANISM IN THE FORMING OF THE ANGLICAN COMMUNION

Several fine summaries of the early history of Anglicanism are available to the interested reader:

"From the Reformation to the Eighteenth Century," by William Haugaard;[4] chapter 1 of *A Brief History of the Episcopal Church*, by David L. Holmes; and of course, Stephen Neill's chapter on Reformation in *Anglicanism*. From them several central themes appear, clearly intertwined. The two of most value to us here are the themes of *settlement* and *basic resources*.

SETTLEMENT AND ESTABLISHMENT

Settlement refers to the English struggle to find a way to have a Church of England established, widely comprehensive and national in scope. This struggle occupied England from the accession of Henry VIII to the Toleration Act of 1689. When it began there was no question that there was but one church in England and one Monarch who was governor of the entire realm, and that state and church were bound together. When it was over there were many churches, and the monarchy was on its way to becoming the symbol of the nation rather than the true governor of either church or state.

The principles of this settlement were laid out during the reign of Elizabeth I. The notion of a "national church that could unite all Catholic-minded English men and women who were willing to stop short of recognizing the authority of the pope and all Protestant-minded citizens who were willing to accept bishops"[5] was articulated. The Thirty-nine Articles of 1571 helped to place the Church of England in a middle way, and theologians, notably Richard Hooker, developed a polity for this Church of England.

The problem is that the Elizabethan Settlement did not hold. With the queen's death, the whole thing almost unraveled, and when it was stitched back together after the reestablishment of the monarchy there was one major difference in the product. Where before there had been a single nation and a single church, there was now a nation with many churches. There was still a national church established and supported by law, but there was no longer one English church. Now there was the "Church of England," and other churches in England as well. Because the church of England was established (paid for by taxes), it could think of itself as *the* English church. But more and more dissenters and "papists" knew better. We should note this pluralism, because when the English went overseas they took not the Church of England, but a plurality of churches. From the recipient's point of view, the English were not all of the same persuasion, and the Anglican Church was only one of a variety of possibilities.

In an odd way there was something wonderfully reforming about pluralism as the natural environment for churches in the Anglican Communion. It meant that the Reformation worked—that the human heart, mind, and soul might find refuge in the Word of God without the incrustations of specific ecclesiastical interpretation. But it also meant that no where in the world would Anglicans find themselves as truly established as they were in England.

BASIC RESOURCES: THE BOOK OF COMMON PRAYER AND THE BIBLE

The Reformation effort to place Holy Scripture in the hands of the people—in their own languages—was a revolutionary activity. It is a prime example of what can happen when people have both the freedom to receive information and access to it in their own language. The assumptions that such access would be beneficial rested on confidence in the faith-enabling power of scripture and in the abilities of the human mind to comprehend. Putting the Bible into people's hands said something about the power of the Bible and about the power of the reader's mind. Humanism, or at least its respect for the abilities of the human mind, had its nest at the heart of the Reformation.

Still, for there to be anything like a comprehensive faith able to bridge Catholic and Protestant sensibilities, it would be immensely helpful to have the scriptures in an agreed-on form and translation; hence the efforts which produced the Authorized Version of the Bible. There might be wide disagreements as to what scripture meant, but there might be reasonable agreement on a translation. The work was successful, and wherever the English went from 1611 on, the Authorized, or "King James," Version of the Bible accompanied them.

The importance of the Authorized Version was that it provided a sense of some unity among all but Roman Catholics, if not in church polity and practice, at least in the words of scripture. It also affirmed the primacy of literacy among the skills to be encouraged among the faithful. This affirmation led not only to the formation of schools and colleges in which English was taught, but also to translations of scripture into other languages some of which, until then, had no written form at all.

The Book of Common Prayer offered another model for comprehension and unity. By having prayers in a language understood by the people, and a single book in which was laid out the order and content of common prayer in churches, the Church of England affirmed a principle of *accessibility*. It made worship less a matter of "hocus pocus" and more an instrument of empowerment. It also affirmed change as morally appropriate. In the Anglican churches scattered across the world there was now a book which in its preface held that "there was never any thing by the wit of man so well devised or so sure established, which in continuance of time hath not been corrupted. . . ." Those who read this understood, and found new courage to become churches in their own right and peoples of self-governance.

The content of the Book of Common Prayer affirmed ordered daily prayer, the sacraments, and orders of ministry with bishops as chief pastors. It did so in ways that it was hoped would serve a single church for a single nation. That did not happen, but at least it did assure that within the Church of England there would be the use of this one book. So, again, the hoped-for conformity of the whole nation was not to be; but the uniformity within the Established church was more or less possible.

The Book of Common Prayer was very much an instrument of "location." That is, it had its reason for being in the particulars of time and space. We speak of "the Book of Common Prayer," but it is important to remember that within the first two hundred years there were several, each molded to its location in history. For most of the period of missionary expansion the book was that of 1662, but as users became aware of the difference in their location from England, they would change its content and form. One historian has called the Book of Common Prayer an "incarnational Book."[6] It may be that it is in its theology and spirit incarnational, but it was also incarnational in that its development was "enfleshed" in the specifics of time and space.

The Authorized Version of the Bible and the Book of Common Prayer were not only primary products of the Reformation in England, they were among the most specifically Anglican artifacts to circulate throughout the world. And they carried with them the germ of a hope that was not realized at home—that there might be a comprehensive and settled faith.

By the time the English began to be a power in the world, a comprehensive established national church in England was no longer a reality. Yet the hope for that comprehensiveness provided Anglican churches with a unique sense of self among the reformed churches. Anglicanism did not view itself as a confessional church, but as an established one. Instead of identifying itself as a righteous remnant, it rested its sense of self and its hopes on common prayer and fairly translated scriptures, on a faith received in tradition, and on reason as a God-given resource.

Anglicanism provided the newly forming Anglican churches with remarkable tools: a Bible, a Prayer Book, sacraments, bishops, a sense of comprehensiveness, and a desire to conform practice to location. The receivers of these gifts would make use of them in ways that could not have been imagined by the Church of England in its struggles.

NOTES ON ANGLICANISM AS EXPERIENCED BY ITS RECEIVERS

A history of the Anglican Communion from the viewpoint of those outside England would likely be quite different from an English-centered history of Anglicanism. In the first place, it would begin with a description of how the English got themselves to other countries, rather than with an explanation of how the faith got to England. Of course that history is mixed. There would have been no such thing as the Anglican Communion, had there not been some sort of adventure—a moving out. A history of the Anglican Communion from the standpoint of the receivers of Anglicanism might well begin with observations about the character of adventure in the modern world.

Adventure in the modern world is a product of corporate greed, individual need for opportunity and liberty, and the conjunction of the full development of several technological advances.[7] The mounting of expeditions and the establishment of settlements required the accumulation of capital and personnel, companies and companions. Chaplains accompanied the adventurers, but almost entirely for the benefit of the adventurers and the companies they represented. Unlike the Roman Catholics, who had taken on new tasks in mission in the sixteenth century, Anglicans and other Protestants did very little to proclaim the gospel in "foreign parts" until the end of the seventeenth century.

In the East and West Indies and in the American colonies we seem to get the first English efforts to bring the gospel to people other than their own colonialists and merchants. New World English charters for colonization of the seventeenth century began to speak of bringing natives to Christ. But European Protestant mission work in any force would await "the emergence of the movement called pietism. . . .The principles of pietism are the demand for personal conversion and for holiness, close fellowship in the Society, and responsibility for witness."[8] Deliberate mission by the Church of England can generally be dated from the establishment of the first two mission societies at the turn of the eighteenth century: the Society for the Promotion of Christian Knowledge (SPCK) and the Society for the Propagation of the Gospel in Foreign Parts (SPG). Both exhibited elements of this pietism. Either by commission, as in the case of SPG and SPCK missionaries, or by accident of personal inclination, as in the case of some chaplains, by the middle of the eighteenth century there were Anglican ministers and churches throughout the world. As Anglican clergy, these missionaries were men under authority. SPG and SPCK missionaries were accountable both to their Societies and to the Bishop of London. English chaplaincies had less clear lines of accountability to London, but were at least accountable to the company that held Royal Charter.

By the late eighteenth century there were churches in the colonies whose members had lived all their lives in these new locations. The beginning of what would become the Anglican Communion is marked by concerns about the relation of these new churches to the home church. The issues seemed fairly straightforward. As church communities began to identify their new locations as home, they came to view the English Church and its organizations as distant. As these communities began to reach out to others—whether to the unchurched or Free-Church English, or to those thought of as foreigners, heathen, or natives—their membership began to include persons that had no real stake in England, its customs, or its laws. As colonies became independent, and as nations became more assertive of their separateness from the British, it became important for churches to claim this separateness as well.

From 1750 to 1850 much effort was made to identify the basis on which separate Anglican churches might be established outside England. Anglicanism is a way of being the church that has now more than 1700 years of experience with which to work, but the emerging notions of ecclesial life that would characterize the Anglican Communion drew primarily on the corporate, nationalist, and individualist sensibilities of the beginning of the modern era in England.

I believe a history of the Anglican Communion should be written which would be begin with "case studies" from these churches. In doing so, many Anglican theological and ecclesial concerns would be reflected. They would appear, however, not as elements of a hard-won effort to work out a "settlement" or establish a church, concerns which arose before modernity took hold. Rather, they would appear in the context of a modern worldview or paradigm.

It would be well beyond the scope of this book, and well beyond my abilities, to write such a history. But it may be useful to give some examples of the cases that would be important to such a history and, in noting them, to signal the ongoing issues of Anglicanism that have reappeared in the development of a modern understanding of the Anglican Communion.

CASE STUDIES IN THE DEVELOPMENT OF THE COMMUNION

THE EAST INDIA COMPANY: CHURCH IN THE MISSION OF COMMERCE

Elizabeth I chartered the East India Company as a business venture in 1600. Beginning in 1607 there were chaplains appointed to serve the needs of the members of the company. To a large extent, the chaplaincies served British citizens overseas. As I have said above, there is little to suggest that during this period there was much missionary work among the native people. During the century, individual chaplains began to apply themselves to making the tools of Anglicanism useful in location. Near the end of the 1600s, the Book of Common Prayer was translated into Portuguese and used by people of mixed Indian and European descent in parts of India.

The Book of Common Prayer of 1662 also recognized the possibility of baptizing "the Natives. . .and others converted to the faith."[9] Toward the end of the century those who were to serve as chaplains with the East India Company were required to learn Portuguese and "the native language," to the end that there might be work for conversion.[10] But for most of the seventeenth century it was company chaplains, not missionaries, who came to India, and most of them had little to do with Indians as "real" people—that is, as worthy candidates for evangelical engagement.

English historians might explain the lack of mission interest in a variety of ways, but what might an Indian historian say about that period? What might seem to be benign missionary neglect could also be seen as insulting. And perhaps, if we are indeed known by our fruits, the whole thing might really confirm that the English were completely and unabashedly there to make money and build an empire.

Pritam B. Santram has written a short essay, "Mission of the Church in the Indian Context," which gives an Indian perspective on

European and Anglican mission activity.[11] In this essay there is no mention of seventeenth-century Anglican activity. Anglican mission begins with the SPG and SPCK and the new pietism that energized them. Santram said about the goals of these societies, "To put it bluntly, the frontier of their mission was the religion of other people."[12] An addendum might be that, in the absence of any such societies or mission, the English simply did not know or care what Indians believed. The beginning awareness of the religion of the English might well have been that it was *for the English*, who after all were not here to engage Indians at all.

THE DECISION FOR MISSION TO "FOREIGN PARTS"

At the turn of the eighteenth century, the two English societies for mission were formed: the SPCK in 1696 and the SPG in 1701. Both were clear signs that members of the church were willing to form corporations for the promotion of their interest, goals and mission, just as the companies of merchants had done a hundred years earlier.

Both societies were created primarily to raise the level of religious knowledge and piety among English peoples in foreign parts, but both quickly expanded these goals to include other people already in those "foreign" places. SPCK worked both to raise the level of Christian learning among its own, and to bring the good news to those who did not know or have it. SPG began as an effort to provide ministry and sacrament to English congregations overseas. It quickly grew to include the provision of ministry and sacrament to some who did not speak English at all.

The societies grew to reflect various elements of *traditional* Anglicanism in a now more religiously pluralistic England. At a time when Deists were claiming that religion primarily served the cause of virtue, the societies had as their mission the promoting and propagation of the knowledge and practice of the faith as received from the ancient church. The societies were in some sense conserving, bringing a fairly consistent and comprehensive reformed catholic faith to communities and people throughout the world.[13]

The advantage of this conservative style was obvious: the church had an authority not totally dependent on existing governments or companies.[14]

It was after all the custodian of the Bible and the Prayer Book. It represented something substantial from the country of origin. The disadvantage was almost devastating: If it was conservative, custodial and *English*, could it ever be really "enfleshed" in these new locations?

Toward the middle of the eighteenth century this issue came to a head. It became increasingly clear that an essential element of Anglicanism was not present in Anglican churches overseas—bishops. Without local episcopal ministry, bishops were simply irrelevant. Worse than irrelevant, the same conserving tendencies that accompanied Anglican mission made it difficult to understand what a bishop was, outside the context of England, where they carried in their combined church and state roles the remnant of the hope of a comprehensive established church. The problem was this: a church faithful to the order of the ancient church would have bishops, but having bishops meant (as far as experience could indicate) establishment, with all its taxes for the support of churches and clergy, and potentially autocratic episcopal styles modeled on the monarchy. That was intolerable, yet bishops also seemed necessary. What could be done?

Anglicanism was certainly seen in the American colonies as conservative, sympathetic to the monarchy, and hierarchical. But Anglican churches were to a large extent freed from actual hierarchical oversight by bishops, often inventive in missionary spirit, and open to independence movements both in the society and church. Still, these churches assumed that having bishops was an essential ecclesial feature. The Prayer Book, after all, said so. The question was how to have them.

Again, an English historian might well look at the difficulties of providing episcopal oversight locally and see one set of reasons. But how might an American see this same question?

The solution in the American colonies was found when necessity became the mother of invention once again. The independence of the United States of America forced the issue of an episcopate for the United States, while at the same time revealing the major social objection to bishops—that they might have governmental roles as the chief ministers of an establishedreligion.

America had been the refuge for many driven out of England in bad times of religious persecution, and for them any talk of bishops was anathema. For the many parishioners who had come to appreciate self-rule of their churches, bishops were not good news either. It is important to remember, however, that in the face of all the pressure *not* to have bishops, the Prayer Book, and priests in America, the practice of religion in Anglican parishes had still conveyed Anglicanism's preference for episcopal polity. A way was continually sought, and finally found, to express that preference. The SPG and other societies in England failed to find a solution. But the solution was found in Scotland. There the understanding of episcopacy was not bound to establishment. The Scottish Episcopal Church could more clearly affirm what bishops were understood to be in Anglicanism—instruments for comprehensive and orthodox faith. And so the Scottish Episcopal Church consecrated a bishop for the United States, Samuel Seabury.

The Anglican Communion is often described as a fellowship. If so, the mutuality between the Scottish Episcopal Church and the emergent Episcopal Church in the United States was a strong precursor to that fellowship. The efforts to adapt the episcopate to local conditions constitute an American "case study" in the history of the Anglican Communion.

Two years after Seabury's consecration in Scotland (1784), the English Parliament passed an act which allowed the consecrations of bishops who would be outside the jurisdiction of English ecclesiastical and civil authority. In the next several years new bishops—two for the United States, one for Nova Scotia, and one for Quebec—were consecrated. Then, after a lull, new consecrations for British colonies and elsewhere began again in 1814. The episcopate was now self-sustaining in the Anglican Communion outside England.[15]

In Anglican Communion history, these events are notable because they established the principle that would replace a venerable idea of Anglicanism—the notion of establishment. The remnant of the Anglican ideal of a truly comprehensive church was the established church. Episcopal oversight, like monarchical oversight, was increasingly limited by growing pluralism in faith and growing democratic aspirations, but it had remained for Anglicanism an assumed characteristic of the establishment. Now, for the first time since the articulation of Anglican polity, bishops were ordained who did not exercise their ministries within an established church. The Chicago-Lambeth Quadrilateral of

1886–1888 would define this new understanding of the episcopate as "the Historic Episcopate, locally adapted in the methods of its administration to the varying need of the nations and people called of God into the Unity of His Church"[16]

MEETING TOGETHER: THE CALLING OF THE FIRST LAMBETH CONFERENCE

By the mid-nineteenth century there were some 150 Anglican bishops around the world. The differences in their understandings of polity were very real, and sometimes both vexing and embarrassing. New synodical forms were arising, some in colonies of England. What, for example, would be the relation of the Church of England and the Archbishop of Canterbury to the primates and people of the Church in New Zealand or the Church in South Africa? How might these Anglican bishops carry out mission in a way true to the spirit of Anglicanism, yet true to location and time?

The Church of Canada put forth the idea of a general synod of Anglican bishops, and in 1867 a meeting of bishops was held at the Archbishop of Canterbury's invitation. From the standpoint of Anglican Communion history, it is important to note that the impetus for meeting came from outside England, and that its role was defined by the desire for mutuality in discussion rather than by synodical politics. The Lambeth Conference has since become a touchstone for mutuality within the communion. It was never envisioned in the beginnings of Anglicanism, yet in important ways it acknowledged and conformed to the idea of episcopal governance in location. The declaration that "the Bishop of Rome hath no jurisdiction in this Realm of England" (The thirty-seventh of the Articles of Religion) opened the same principle to application later in reference to England. Thus, the Bishop of Canterbury, it could be argued, has no jurisdiction in the synodical life of the church in any constituent province of the Anglican Communion. The form the Lambeth Conferences have taken affirms a principle never envisioned in Anglicanism's beginnings but clearly appropriate to its spirit.

The development of the Lambeth Conference is a case study in the development of mutuality among Anglican churches. It suggests the care with which reformed catholic ideals were considered.

WORKING FOR UNION: THE CHICAGO LAMBETH QUADRILATERAL

Another case study relates to the development of, and value placed on, the Lambeth Quadrilateral (1888). This document, almost a manifesto really, grew out of the Anglican Communion's—not particularly the Church of England's—agenda. This fact sets in context its purpose and the issues it addresses. It was by intention a strategy for engagement on the issue of the reunion of churches, and grew out of an Episcopal Church proposal.

In the United States the ecclesial issue at stake in the latter part of the nineteenth century was not that of dealing with an already existing established church, but rather with the attempt to visualize what a church for the nation might look like. It raised a post-denominational vision of the church in an age of greatly multiplying churches and sects and at a time (at least in the U.S.) of low societal norms and morals. In one sense it was a way of asking precisely the reverse of the question of establishment that had plagued England. Here the issue was whether there was any way for Christianity to have a united voice for the good of the people and the good of the nation.

The national church idea, first proposed by William Reed Huntington, was a way to continue this sense of a church for the whole people *without* establishment. As a matter of ecumenical faithfulness it was thought that the vision should be that of Christians in place becoming the church—not of the Anglican or Episcopal Church in some form we might envision, but the church already in place, the church of the people or nation. The Chicago-Lambeth Quadrilateral was the end result of this vision.

It was the profound sense of the provisional, and indeed broken, character of the separated churches that led the bishops at Lambeth to adopt and modify the American proposal and publish the Quadrilateral. In terms of Anglican Communion history, the Lambeth Quadrilateral stands as a statement of the willingness of Anglican bishops to exercise authority provisionally, against the day when the church might take new form.

The Quadrilateral opened the way for a different sort of ecumenical discussion, one in which episcopacy would be offered as a gift for the good of the church, rather than a given of established religion. It also cleared the agenda for union or reunion. No longer would the Thirty-Nine Articles carry confessional-church weight. They were not mentioned in the Quadrilateral. There the point of contact for discussion was the ancient creeds, not the confessional statements of the Reformation period.

The Lambeth Quadrilateral, presented as a case history in the development of the Anglican Communion, is again something viewed quite differently by various Anglican historians and theologians. It would be very helpful to have the observations of Anglicans throughout the world on just what the Quadrilateral has meant in the context of the various provinces. My sense is that a history of the Anglican Communion written, for example, in India or China would look at its meaning, usefulness, and ecclesial value in a way very different from the way some English and American writers would look at it.

An attempt to survey all the most useful cases for a history of the Anglican Communion would go well beyond what I can do here. But at least I hope the suggestion of shifting the historical viewpoint from England to the Communion is a useful challenge. I look forward to reading such a history. For our purposes here it is enough to suggest that a vision for the Anglican Communion also requires our care about vantage point. Vision is a matter of location as well as insightfulness.

TWO TWENTIETH-CENTURY CONCERNS IN THE ANGLICAN COMMUNION

Before turning to the specific themes which I believe inform a vision for the future of the Anglican Communion, I want to examine briefly two continuing issues in Anglican Communion thought. They could be seen at the first meeting of Lambeth, and they continue to this day. They are the issues of *mutuality* and *establishment*. They remain in tension in the Anglican Communion because the Church of England has not solved its own internal issues of establishment, and all the rest of us have not solved the problem of being Anglican without being English.

MUTUAL RESPONSIBILITY AND INTERDEPENDENCE

In 1963 a remarkable document was published, the results of the Anglican Congress held in Toronto. It was titled *Mutual Responsibility and Interdependence in the Body of Christ (MRI)*. While many of its specific strategies have been superseded by subsequent Anglican Communion practice, it brought certain understandings of right mission practice to center stage for Anglicans. In particular, it spelled out for its time the primary issues of being a fellowship (*koinonia*) in which Christ was the head, and in which all practices (including roles within the Body) are subject to the provisionality of interdependence. Simply put, what *MRI* did was to say that Anglicans understand the relationships between their churches to be one of mutuality, in which the roles of churches are determined by their interdependence, not by artificial pictures of "older" or "younger," "richer" or "poorer," churches.

Anticipating and following on the Toronto Congress, a number of papers and monographs were written enlarging on the themes of *MRI*. A survey of several of them is useful, because they give some sense of practice and self-understanding within the Communion.

The Anglican Communion in Christendom, by A. E. J. Rawlinson, was published in 1960, on the eve of the Toronto Congress. Much of what Rawlinson writes concerns Church of England ecumenical matters, and indeed his primary effort is to show where he believes both Anglican and Church of England commitments are likely to go. He begins this short work with one of the most balanced sketches I have read of the development of the Anglican Communion. At the close Rawlinson says, "It is by no means certain that *Ecclesia Anglicana* as such ought to continue indefinitely to exist as a separate 'Communion' in Christendom, though its members believe that its distinctive witness will long be required."[17]

Rawlinson spelled out what he considered to be the basic theological issues concerning ecumenical work toward reunion. In relation to those themes, he makes the following observations:

(1) Schism is an internal matter to the church, and therefore all communions in the church are at fault.[18]

(2) Holiness is both an internal matter of individuals (purity), and an external matter for the whole church (sacraments).[19]

(3) The claims of catholicity are available to all Christians as a matter *of the future* rather than the past;[20] "commissioning to ministry is bestowed through those who already hold it, but it [the ministry itself] comes from the Risen, Reigning, and Present Lord Himself."[21]

(4) The ecumenical stance of Anglicans is thus open to humility in relation to other churches, to respect for the sacramental life of other churches, to catholicity as a matter of the future, and to interpretation regarding episcopacy.[22]

Rawlinson argued on the basis of these theological observations that Anglicans can and ought to be open to the widest sort of conversation toward unity. Most importantly, he suggested that regional schemes for unity (the churches in Pakistan and Ceylon, various plans of union with in England) must all go forward. They might all be sources of union and division at the same time, but given the Anglican theological stances he outlined, it was his sense that Anglicans have a particular ecumenical role to play. We must be willing and able to stretch as we can, so that the catholicity of the future is somehow prefigured in the present. The Anglican Communion

> is humbly conscious of what may well prove to be a unique vocation to play a distinctive part in the bringing together of the several branches of Christendom. Its platform from this point of view, is what has become known as the Chicago-Lambeth Quadrilateral.[23]

Stephen Bayne, Jr., then Executive Officer of the Anglican Communion and a principal architect of *MRI*, wrote a foreword to a short monograph by Dewi Morgan published in connection with the international Anglican Congress in Toronto in August 1963.[24] The monograph was a glimpse into the thinking behind *MRI*, before the document was actually written. As such, it retains a purity of motive unrelated to the doctrines that arose from *MRI* itself. Bishop Bayne said in his preface,

> The vocation of an Anglican is inescapably and sometimes painfully and always profoundly ecumenical. We are driven by our own deepest insights and gifts into the fight to find and manifest an unimaginable unity, a unity already given us in the wonderful and terrible unities of God's creation and loving redemption of us, which has never fully been grasped and held by men.[25]

This ecumenical perspective was reiterated in the author's own foreword:

> It is my conviction that if Anglicans are to be obedient to the call of God to unity and are to be active partners in its pursuit, they must examine their treasurers, if any. Just what do they have to bring in return for the gifts they will receive from the other Churches? . . .What use has God for the Anglican Communion?[26]

Morgan saw the questions of freedom and authority as central to the missionary task. He said that

> Our job is to keep asking God to show us what sort of a future he wants for it, and in the light of that to ask him what is the next step he wants us to take. . . .The concept of all the nations actively responding to God's word in Christ by relating it to their own conscience, reason and experience is surely one which carries any Christian mind into very green and lush pastures. We have in the past deprived ourselves of much vision and encouragement by not relating this idea to all our missionary work.[27]

The result of this understanding of freedom of conscience, reason, and experience is very much what became the issue of mutuality in *MRI*. The emphasis in *MRI* is on action *in the Body of Christ*. As a body of believers, in various national and regional churches, Anglicans participate in the Incarnation as members a single whole, the Body of Christ. The principle sign of that organic union is communion rather than governance. We are ordered by our willingness to see ourselves as part of a whole, not by being constituted for some other end. Morgan saw this as the basis for the Anglican Communion's understanding of itself:

> You must have more than one entity if there is to be communion. You cannot share with yourself. The Anglican Communion is not a world church, but a world fellowship of churches. The classical statement on this point was at Lambeth 1930: "This (Anglican Communion) is a commonwealth of Churches without a central constitution: it is a federation without a federal government. It has come into existence without any deliberate policy. . . . They (the Churches) are in the idiom of our fathers, 'particular or

national' Churches and they repudiate any idea of a central authority other than Councils of Bishops."[28]

Since some form of engagement must happen for there to be organic unity, Morgan acknowledged the need to provide a basis for relationship. He did so by speaking of family ties. He began with a wonderful statement of the problem known to any who participate in Anglican gatherings:

> To western man, with his passion for organization, and his apparent conviction that nothing can work well unless you have administrative tidiness, the Anglican Communion must surely be a cogent proof that the doctrine of the survival of the fittest has very little validity in spiritual matters. The last thing which the congeries of Anglican Christians can claim is any mechanical efficiency. By most natural laws, the Anglican Communion simply should not exist. Yet it does. To the question "What holds it together?" there can be only one answer: God. And one frequently gets the impression that God must want it pretty powerfully; else it would have disappeared long ago.[29]

Morgan went on to suggest that the mechanisms for sharing who we are sufficed, provided the sense of belonging together was in place. And that sense is provided in the strength of our awareness that "there is One Lord, one Faith, one Baptism, shared by multifarious peoples divided by a thousand earthly barriers."[30]

JOHN HEUSS AND SOME SUPPOSED IMPLICATIONS OF THE TORONTO MANIFESTO

In 1963 it might have been the clear intention of those involved not to have *MRI* lead to some sort of "world church." But by 1965, when John Heuss wrote *The Implications of the Toronto Manifesto,* he argued that it is precisely a world church that is needed, and that *MRI* ultimately would lead to its formation. The monograph is a collection of three sermons he delivered at the Seabury-Western Theological Seminary, in which he addressed the implications of the Toronto statement.

There is considerable wisdom in these sermons, along with a good deal of mistaken or deliberately obscured information. We should take note of them, however, because Heuss forthrightly called for a centralized

Anglican Communion "office" from which mission and ministry for the whole communion might be organized, and an international system of governance provided for Anglicans. Heuss's arguments are popularly stated, strong, and cogent, and they represent the case for the projection of American corporate and political processes into the international community of the Anglican Communion. This case has been brought forward again more recently as the communion has grown in size and complexity.

Heuss defined the Anglican Communion as "a section of historical Christianity with branches or provinces located in many different parts of the world. . . ."[31] He began by noting that "no single person and no single central planning group brought about the spread of the Anglican Communion. It is doubtful if any world-encircling Christian missionary effort was ever undertaken so haphazardly."[32]

Two statements, in the first paragraph of his first sermon on the subject, define the matter as far as he was concerned:

(1) the Anglican Communion is a "world-encircling Christian missionary effort," a whole, "a section" of historical Christianity; and

(2) there is no central authority or structure guiding its missionary efforts.

Heuss believed the first of these to be true and the second both true, and in the modern age, lamentable.

> I do not believe that we can afford the old-fashioned, unplanned and uncoordinated missionary outreach of the eighteenth and nineteenth centuries. The very heart of the agony of Anglicanism, which found a voice at the Anglican Congress in Toronto in 1963, was that the old missionary methods were no longer suited to a world where every one had a mutual responsibility to every one else in the Body of Christ.[33]

The need for a new missionary method is clear, he says, but,

> the unanswered question still is how shall mutual responsibility really be implemented in a communion with a history such as ours? I do not believe [realistic answers to this question] will come until we get beyond the concept of ourselves as members of independent national provinces. . . and take the big imaginative leap of believing and acting as

> if the Anglican Communion were one great united Church
> acting with one plan for the whole world mission of Christ.[34]

I believe Heuss's analysis was mistaken. But it would be unnecessary to prove it mistaken if it were not still being argued. The Anglican Communion is not a federation, nor is it even "a section of historical Christianity with branches. . . ." It has no legislative authority, and it is viewed by several other communions as not being a "section" of the tree of the true faith at all.

More accurate is our own Episcopal Church's constitution and canons, which define the Anglican Communion as "a Fellowship" along the lines of the 1930 Lambeth Conference.[35] Far from being federated as to its governance, this community of mutuality is held together by the sharing of the eucharist, a matter of charity. The "section and branch" image is a leftover from the attempt to diagram those churches which are "historical," that is, have apostolic succession or the historic episcopate.

Heuss argued that the Anglican Communion *is* a whole, but a badly governed and managed whole. "It grew," he said, "like Topsy."[36] The object of the present time in the life of the communion, in his mind, was to find the way to provide good governance and management for the future.

Some of Heuss's ideas have been developed further: The Anglican Consultative Council (ACC), the role of Inter-Anglican bodies such as the Theological and Doctrinal Commission, the Mission Agencies Working Group (MISAG), and the widening role of the Secretary General of the Anglican Communion have all developed to meet some of the concerns he first voiced.

Heuss's vision was of "one great communion," which could engage in mission, education, evangelism, and ecumenism on a worldwide level. It was, on some levels, a triumphalist vision. It borrowed much from the American model of the Executive Council of the Episcopal Church, with which he was very familiar, having been on the national staff. But it uncritically assumed that central organization was good and the model for the future. There was, of course, no way for him to visualize networks of people, ideas, cultures, etc., joined together not as a hierarchy but as a matrix. Some of what was needed in terms of organizational vision was simply not addressed at that time. Not until the circle, rather than the pyramid, became an organizational model, would there begin to be anything like the mutuality *MRI* envisioned. It was a model that developed in the church only when women began to have a serious voice.

Heuss's sermons are filled with a vision that to some extent still attracts some who seek to understand and build a solid organization for the Anglican Communion in the future. The vision of a world Anglican church is a way to address the need for authority, but it is not an easy vision for those who love the freedom in which "perfect service" is reserved for our relationship in service to our Lord.

CAUTIONARY TALES OF IRRESPONSIBILITY

At the same time Heuss was preaching the seeming good news of a worldwide Anglican church, Douglas Webster wrote on the possibilities of *Mutual Irresponsibility*.[37] In a small booklet with this title, he outlined some of the difficulties in taking *MRI* and using it as a substitute for thinking things through, or for trying to turn a vision into programs too quickly. Unlike the Toronto manifesto, which had an agenda of its own to promote, *Mutual Irresponsibility* was a cautionary statement, trying to limit ill-formed missionary agendas.

Some of his cautions hold up over time and others do not. He was certainly right to point out that *MRI* was viewed by many as a money-raising scheme. The *Directory of Projects* that soon accompanied the *MRI* manifesto looked surprisingly like a shopping list. That was later corrected by the Partners in Mission proposal that designed consultations as a way of providing a wider viewpoint on mutual analysis of concerns and problems.

Webster had some enduring observations to make about the problems of inviting clergy from other parts of the communion for study or work in the "older churches." Much of what he had to say about companion dioceses has been dealt with well by the actual experience of engagement in that process.

Webster made one suggestion concerning short-term service by Western clergy overseas that still stands as an argument for some sort of *international* mission office in the Anglican Communion:

"The Anglican Communion needs some kind of administrative

machinery for facilitating such exchanges, and it ought to be quite distinct from the existing missionary societies and organizations. This could do much to break down the barriers of ignorance in a new generation of clergy and to create the desire to be mutually responsible."[38]

Webster advocated two things:

(1) "A real exchange of prayer and living agents. . . .Our concern is with the Church of the living God, not with human organization, and the whole testimony of Scripture insists that in the divine community more can be achieved by prayer and dedicated service than by any other means.[39]

(2) That "we realize the severe limitations of money in achieving spiritual results unless it is given in this context of knowledge, prayer and service."[40]

The prayer exchange he proposed has become standardized in the *Anglican Cycle of Prayer*. The living agents wait for new forms of mission sending and receiving. The two together really set this short essay in context: It is a plea to see all matters of mutual responsibility and interdependence as matters of *measured* response.

Webster was trying to caution against unthinking action by missionary enthusiasts and a rush to the easy organizational response of giving money in preference to carefully considered mutual engagement. In the Episcopal Church, both mistakes were, in fact, to follow shortly. In the years following *MRI*, there was an increase in mission personnel sent to former Church of England missionary areas, and this was followed by a long, slow decline in the numbers of missionaries and a gradual decline in funding.[41]

The practice that arose out of this first attempt to state an Anglican Communion-wide understanding of mission was varied. On the one hand, *MRI* focused on the issues of interdependence in ways that changed our attitudes about missionary engagement. On the other hand, *MRI* raised the possibility of an international agency for mission in the Anglican Communion, in which information and decision making would be made on a programmatic level, in a centralized way and for centralized concerns. The potential was that the practice would somehow be at odds with itself. That has quickly become a reality of Anglican Communion life. As a fellowship we are increasingly aware of our mutuality and interdependence. But at the same time there is an increasing awareness that the managerial hierarchies of the churches in the communion that have traditionally "sent" missionaries talk more to each other than to anyone else. So our practice clashes with its own principles.

In the 1960s, *MRI* provided the directives for missionary practice. As we have seen, however, it also raised questions about the coherence and structure of a worldwide communion. There has been considerable practical response to the question of structure, principally in the growing work of the ACC and the establishment of the Primates' Meetings, but the matter of coherence has remained. Indeed it has grown. It has been connected to the issue of Anglican identity, but it is also related to the matter of practice.[42] Mutuality is an art, and the question is whether we as members of the Anglican Communion are any good at its practice.

CONTINUING PROBLEMS OF THE ESTABLISHED CHURCH IN ENGLAND

England has continued to have to wrestle with what it means to be an established church. A number of English writers have tried to address the question of an Anglican doctrine of the church. If there were one that could be agreed on, it would be most helpful.

IS THERE AN ANGLICAN DOCTRINE OF THE CHURCH?

In his essay, "Anglicanism and the Anglican Doctrine of the Church,"[43] Stephen Sykes argues that Anglicans do have a doctrine of the church, and that it is coherent with the Anglican practice of church. Sykes has been a major proponent of a more disciplined approach to Anglicanism, believing that for too long we have hidden behind a sort of warm fuzzy sense of catholic inclusiveness. Sykes does a bit of logic-chopping in his argument against the widely held notion that Anglicans have "no special doctrines." This is, I believe, unfortunate and condescending. But his underlying point is well taken:

> The issue of the authority of the Church of England, and of the churches in communion with her, to declare in the

absence of contemporary Christian unanimity that such-and-such constitutes a sufficient statement of Christian faith is unavoidable. For this right to exist in the way Anglicans believe or assume that it does, it must exist in the church as such. That is to say. . .there must be a theology of the church according to which the churches of the Anglican Communion have the right to make controversial declarations about the extent of the content of the Christian faith. . . .Anglicans, therefore, must have at least one special doctrine of their own.[44]

The "sufficient statement of the Christian faith" that has often been proposed is the Lambeth Quadrilateral. It is the authority of the Lambeth Conference to make such a statement that constitutes, in Sykes's understanding, the beginning point for saying that Anglicans must have a doctrine of the church. Otherwise there would be no authority for the Anglican Communion to make such a statement.

Sykes argues at the same time that the Quadrilateral is not truly a doctrine of the church, rather it is in some way advice on the way to becoming doctrine. He says,

It is both possible and desirable for Anglican theologians to attempt to formulate the Anglican understanding of the church. The Chicago-Lambeth Quadrilateral is no substitute for such an undertaking, and its very ambiguities should illustrate to us the urgency of the task.[45]

He argues that we must get on with the task if we are to be part of wider theological discussions with other churches. It is not a persuasive argument, for its basis is in rather unfortunate logic-chopping on the one hand or in setting up the Chicago-Lambeth Quadrilateral to be something it never claimed to be, namely an official Anglican doctrine of the church. Sykes may be correct to call Anglicans to task about not having worked more on a doctrine of the church, but I believe he is incorrect to suppose that the Lambeth Quadrilateral claimed to be such a doctrine. It was, and is, a pragmatic strategy for working toward union, not a document defining a doctrine.

Sykes states that many Anglican writers have held that Anglicans are not by intention anything but the church universal in a particular place (initially England), and that Anglicanism's understandings of church are those of the earliest "undivided" church.[46] He quite rightly suggests that there are difficulties with this view. But difficulties do not make the position impossible; rather they require more careful work. It is naive to think that there was as a time of unanimity in the church, or that there are decisions that represent the whole church, as opposed to particular parties that carried the day. To the extent that Anglicans claim the theology of an "undivided church," they rely on a myth. At the same time, the wonderful character of tradition is that it does not require such unanimity, but rather reasonably wide common experience.

The naive notion of early church unanimity, and calling that notion *tradition*, is improved by looking at tradition as *experience over time*, that is, as a pragmatic basis for knowledge and belief. Sykes is right to suggest that there can be no naive return to a pure and united past. But that does not undermine the validity of the view that Anglicans need not have a special doctrine of the church, or that Anglicanism relies on the wide experience of the early church.

I believe Sykes fails to state the real agenda for his passionately wanting to have a clear Anglican doctrine of the church. That reason concerns the relation between nation and church—in particular, the problem of the Church of England and its need to admit finally that it is not what it envisions itself to be, the nation at prayer, but rather one denomination among many. It is a Church of England problem, with a self-understanding that would necessitate the "time for Anglican apologetic to rejoin modern theological discussion and cease the pretence of being above the denominations."[47] Sykes, I believe, confuses the critical problem of establishment in England with the wider and, frankly, less pressing question of an Anglican understanding of church. He wants an Anglican doctrine of the church precisely so that it can take its place among the denominations. That may be good or bad, but it is primarily a problem in England.

Elsewhere it is a fact that we are denominationally distinct enough to be separate and separated from others. In the United States, for example, we are not the nation at prayer, and never have been. We do not have or pretend to have a specific doctrine of the church, separate from what we claim is the sufficient doctrine proposed in the common life of the early church. It is sufficient that we are separated out because we do not claim that our distinctness is central. That is to say, most Anglican churches are not established churches.

Sykes challenges Anglican theologians to take seriously what he considers the criticism of other Christians:

> We have to face the uncomfortable fact that traditional Anglican diffidence in presenting its doctrine of the church strikes Christians of other allegiances not as the fruit of modesty, but of pride and fear: pride, in desiring to occupy a place which no other communion in Christendom occupies, and fear of the consequences, internal and external, of having to formulate a responsible account on behalf of a body which has got out of the habit of taking its theology seriously.[48]

His challenge is made at considerable expense. I find it almost inexplicable, and somewhat insulting, that Sykes would suggest that Anglicans do not take their theology seriously. What I think he means is that there may not be too many Anglicans who want to propose a *specific* Anglican theology which, on behalf of the Anglican churches, competes for the hearts and minds of Christians. Perhaps most Anglicans are content to suppose that the church is not finally Anglican, and that the vision and theology we have for the church rests beyond (and perhaps beneath) the forms we have in place at present.

My sense is that Anglicans are not primarily concerned with our own denominational stance, but rather with an understanding—or for that matter, a vision—of the universal church in which Anglicans are only a part. Sykes seems to want Anglicans to develop a doctrine of the church and a more presentable theology as a denomination.

This brings us to the core of the issue. Sykes claims that Anglicans evade the responsibility of maintaining a doctrine of the church. But perhaps that evasion is part of the very fabric of Anglican thought, namely that doctrine is not definitive, but *provisional*. What replaces certain doctrine, then, is the weight of tradition, scripture, and reason, as experienced through the ages. While this may itself constitute a doctrine of the church—the belief that, prior to the return of the Lord, all authority and doctrine is provisional—it at least places the matter in the context of experiential interpretation. Sykes asks that there be more work done on the Anglican doctrine of the church. I think a proper response to his request is to do more work on an Anglican understanding of the provisional character of its own separate ministry, and indeed the ministry of all churches and sects in the time of separation.

THE BAPTISMAL PARADIGM: PAUL AVIS AND THE ISSUE OF MODELING THE CHURCH

An avenue in the search for an Anglican doctrine of the church has been put forward by Paul Avis, following the same lines as Stephen Sykes. Avis suggests that

> an Anglican ecclesiology would have to be the product of research and discussion through the Anglican Communion—a task perhaps for the Inter-Anglican Theological and Doctrinal Commission. . . .The roots of such an Anglican ecclesiology would inevitably have to be discovered in the "theological resources in historical perspective."[49]

The issue of Anglican identity rather than doctrine is at the core of Avis's concern, for he sees doctrine as a means of self-identification. He asks:

> What is distinctive about Anglicanism? What is its peculiar contribution to world Christianity? What can its particular way of being the church teach us? Can it teach us anything about how to respond constructively to the questions that face the church today? What are its prospects for the future?[50]

To have a vocation is a matter of practical consequence. We ask, "What is the person or corporate body being called by God to witness to in the world?" No matter that others are called to other tasks; no matter that the articulation of that call is poorly stated; the only issue of substance is this: Has the one called in fact responded *in practice*? This approach sees Anglicanism as practice, and it defines Anglicans in terms of practice.

The problem is that the effort to identify practice is very much like the effort to identify doctrine. The difference, I would submit, is that practice admits to a fluidity that doctrine cannot. For example, if a doctrinal identity of Anglicans were to be proposed that would require assent to the Thirty-Nine Articles, those who did not so assent would not be Anglicans. But if *practice* were the principle context for identity, we would ask Anglicans about their attitudes about and their understanding of the Thirty-Nine Articles. Those few who had any idea of what we were talking about would let us know what they thought and they would tell us how it influenced their practice. From the rest, we would receive puzzled looks. Out of that exercise we would conclude that the Articles have a real, but limited, place in the thinking of people who call themselves Anglican. We would not even pretend that they constituted a body of doctrine.

But why the search for identity? Who asks for this? Avis admits this problem, with some real eloquence, when he asks who really has much at stake in the search for an Anglican identity.[51] The answer is, very few do. The question of Anglican identity as a matter of *integrity*, he rightly sees as a "domestic matter,"[52] one concerning the Church of England and its continued problem of being in reality a denomination and in state ideology, *the* church. Sykes sees this matter of integrity as being essentially about identity, and Avis notes Sykes's claim "that for a church integrity is equivalent to 'coherent identity.'"[53]

Avis at least widens the discussion of identity and integrity beyond the particulars of the Church of England, by noting that the issue also concerns pluralism in society.

> It is only when the church becomes relativised by the emergence of rival churches, secular belief systems and profane ways of life, that identity becomes an issue. . .in the new relativistic situation of a secular society it is certainly true that there will be no integrity without identity.[54]

So the issue at hand for Avis is that, in the face of religious alternatives in the world (but whom could this surprise except a member of a state church?), one has to know where one stands, and why. That, I believe, throws the matter out of the realm of historical analysis (although that is interesting at times) and into the matter of practice. Avis admits as much when he says,

> Christian identity—and derivatively Anglican identity—is not fixed and unchanging. Like personal and social identity it is fluid, dynamic, vulnerable. It cannot be created at will, it cannot be guaranteed, it does not need to be defended by ideology, it is not in the church's possession. The church's identity is eschatological.[55]

In the end, Anglican identity is a subset of Christian identity. Avis points a way forward in the search for Christian identity, and finally puts to rest any further search for Anglican identity or an Anglican doctrine of the church when he states:

> In my view, the way ahead is to take the baptismal paradigm as our guide, to liberate the inner dynamic of Christian reality in the church—our incorporation into Christ through baptism by the word and the Holy Spirit—and to ask: What is essential to Christianity? How do historical determinants and canonical structures stand in relation to that? What is it that is enough to make us Christians and communicants in our own churches? And then to ask the further question: Is not that enough to provide the grounds for intercommunion? And is not intercommunion the only sound ecclesiological basis for further steps to unity?[56]

So in some ways the flag that went up calling for an Anglican doctrine of the church is struck down precisely on the point that Anglicanism ought rather to look beyond itself to the unity for which our Lord prayed, and a church in which we see ourselves as a contributing part.

Avis begins by asking about Anglican identity so that we can take our place at the ecumenical table as full partners, both domestically in England and in the world Christian community. He ends by returning, not to peculiar Anglican doctrine, but to an emerging general Anglican practice—that all who are baptized are welcomed to receive communion. It is taking a while to get there, but that practical matter is all that finally counts, for it establishes that being Anglican is provisional, being a product of time and experience, and that Anglicanism has a vocation to witness to an openness which it hopes to see encouraged.

THE PRESS FOR COHERENCE

A wide discussion of the lack of Anglican identity has been initiated again with the publication in 1993 of *The Transformation of Anglicanism*. William Sachs, the author, sees this book as part of the continuing debate fomented by Stephen Sykes in *The Integrity of Anglicanism* in 1978. Sachs claims that Sykes

> has elicited widespread agreement that the churches in com-
> munion with the Church of England lack assurance of their
> identity and mission. . . .Anglicans have no coherent sense
> of identity and no apparent means to resolve their uncer-
> tainty. An uncertainty over the Church's nature has arisen
> under the impact of modern circumstances.[57]

Not only does Sachs accept this contention of Sykes as fact, he associates the so-called crisis with the impact of modern circumstances, by
which I believe he must mean the end of *modernity*.

Sachs's unfolding of Anglican thought on a variety of theological
and historical matters is invaluable for its contextualizing of what was
done and thought. But I remain unconvinced by his contention that the
church's central concern is its identity as Anglican. In the first place,
which church is concerned? Almost all the writers on this subject and
interested parties are English or concerned with Church of England
issues. Very few voices from elsewhere in the communion are heard.

In the second place, the concern about the end of modernity is not
a specifically Anglican one. The fact that many denominations are not
equipped to deal with the post-modern period is a product largely of the
fact that our churches, as separated communities, spring from the
beginnings of the modern period. To the extent that identity is the
church's issue in these times, it is the church's issue because the whole
of western culture is having a nervous breakdown. This is a time, I
believe, for Anglicans, along with other faithful people, to take the
moral bankruptcy of the west seriously and finally determine to become
truly disestablished. In this effort we will be aided, as Anglicans, by
being part of a *koinonia,* a community of mutuality, whose direction
more and more comes from post- or extra-modern leadership.

It seems to me that we are living in a time when Christians, not to
mention Anglicans as Christians, have to live into a "horizontal" rootedness—as a current living and working community—not into a "vertical" rootedness of the historical past. We must turn to the *practice* of
Anglicanism, rather than to its sense of *self-identification,* if we are to
find out something about the vocation of the Anglican Communion.

Sachs admits some of this. He notes of Frederick Maurice that he
"sensed that the Church must evolve an identity rooted in praxis *in*

mission. He anticipated the transformation of Anglicanism with a comprehension no other figure achieved."[58] The problem is that the transformation is just now beginning to be felt in Anglicanism. And as it takes place, those who are guided by the vertical rootedness of history react with abject horror.

These are not easy times for Anglicans, who are divided by genuine breaks with the past—the ordination of women, the radical change in the ethnic character of the Book of Common Prayer, the end of white and colonial domination of the direction of mission and church life, the massive reclamation of the rights of the baptized. These are all affirmations of the horizontal in a church whose life has almost always been vertical in its approach till now.

For example, the office of bishop, seen primarily as a guarantor of succession, could be viewed horizontally, from the standpoint of praxis and practice. Sachs noted the effort by the American church in the nineteenth century to develop the episcopate in a horizontal way. Rather than as a guarantor of historical continuity, the episcopate was seen as the focus of church mission and expansion.[59] One of the results of this was the development of the missionary episcopate, a specifically American innovation.[60] This is precisely one of the points of the Chicago-Lambeth Quadrilateral. It proposes the episcopacy as a device for governance and ecumenical engagement, a practical and immediate issue for the church, not as a monarchical method of title transfer.[61]

Religious tradition certainly has a central and honored place in the present and future of Anglicanism, but for reasons not related particularly to the maintenance of various remnants of modernity. The modern stress on the separation of knowledge and belief is overcome not by moving historically to some point in the past where belief had the upper hand, but by coming to a new understanding of the matrix of events, ideas, beliefs, thoughts, feelings, suggestions, visions, etc., that shape our actions. Religious tradition can be a means of informing us of the wrestling, and the best and worse results of that, so that we can incorporate that experience into our own. Here again, the value of tradition is not, as Sachs contends, that it "guarantees the validity of the Church's ministry."[62] Rather, tradition informs us in valuable and quite open ways about experiences already had in the community. It is important to note that in the post-modern era, and certainly until some new overarching scheme is devised, there is no authority that guarantees the validity of the church's ministry, *save practice.*

Among the remnants of the "old" vision of Anglicanism is that of the identification of the Church of England with empire. Sachs provides a fascinating parallel between Anglicanism as a confederation of churches and the rise of the British Commonwealth.[63] What is interesting, at the end of the period of modernity, is that the commonwealth, just as the British Empire before it, is of less and less consequence. The links between former colonies, and alliances they make with parallel former colonial powers, are every bit as important as the continuing commonwealth. That parallel is valid for the Anglican Communion as well—witness the meetings of leaders of the "Churches of the South."

Roland Allen was seen by Sachs as particularly helpful in trying to trace the threads of method, theology, and missiology as we move beyond the modern era:

> Allen became a great theorist who stressed that mission should not perpetuate particular forms of authority, but should convey a quality of the divine Spirit from whose benefits none was excluded. Allen believed that the mission Church should evolve from individual experience of the Spirit toward a corporate expression of it. . . .Christianity therefore was a principle of life looking for practical realizations. Missionary work should emulate Christ's Incarnation, where God's essence assumed human form.[64]

The pragmatic character of this approach rings true to post-modern developments in mission—contextual ministry and understanding of scripture, Spirit-led, locally affirmed, practically realized. Allen to some extent caused it, of course, but history has borne him out. All of this, too, suggests that waiting in the wings of the houses where the arguments about authority are taking place are those who see the search for that authority and special identity as unnecessary.

From a missionary perspective, there is no future for the Anglican churches as denominationally separate parts of the broken body. That is quite different from denying that there is a future *for what has been modeled* by Anglican churches, for at least some of what we have loved so much about our church is grounded in a sense of *koinonia,* with a special stress on common prayer and sacraments, that will outlive its current forms. And much of what is present in the mutuality of the Anglican Communion will serve the future of the Christian church well.

My sense is that Sachs knows this: "Modernity has proven to be both Anglicanism's glory and its frustration, a paradox without apparent means of resolution."[65] That is precisely the point: paradoxes do not have resolution. They are not supposed to have resolution. They are meant to be experienced and learned from. Perhaps the churches to come and their communities of mutuality will tell our story as their own.

TWO CASE STUDIES IN THE PRESS FOR COHERENCE

While Archbishop Tutu can remark that "Anglicanism is very lovely, but very, very untidy,"[66] and perhaps think that a reasonable state of affairs, the press for coherence goes on in other quarters. Sometimes it concerns doctrine, sometimes, as in the following examples, it concerns issues of structure and mission-consciousness. These issues seem small, and indeed, in relation to the great issues of faith and practice, they are. Yet these seemingly small things have odd consequences.

(A) A Case Study on Structure: Titles for the Presiding Bishop of the Episcopal Church

Stephen Neill noted in *Anglicanism* that

> The chief bishop of the American Church is known as the presiding bishop. He is not a metropolitan, and has no authority in any diocese which has a bishop of its own. . . . This is an arrangement without precedent, and must be judged to be a very bad one. . . .It is hoped that the American Church will recognize that this anomalous situation is undesirable. . . .[67]

He also noted in a footnote that the Presiding Bishop "is therefore, properly, 'The Right Reverend,' and not 'The Most Reverend.'"[68] Since the *Episcopal Church Annual* and the General Convention *Journal* both now title the Presiding Bishop "The Most Reverend," something has happened in the past thirty years concerning the perception of the Presiding Bishop's role both in the Episcopal Church and in the Anglican Communion. The story of these changes tells us something about the consequences of the press for coherence.

In 1967 there first appeared in the Constitution of the Episcopal Church a *Preface*, in which the Episcopal Church was placed in the context of the Anglican Communion. This change came through resolution from the Mutual Responsibility Committee to the Committee on Structure of the General Convention in 1964 for first passage. At that same 1967 Convention the duties of the Presiding Bishop, in Canon 2.4 were changed to a list that began, "The Presiding Bishop is the Chief Pastor. . . ."

It is no accident that these changes occurred as soon as possible after the Anglican Congress in Toronto. Until that Congress there was no particular inter-Anglican need to assert that the Presiding Bishop had any metropolitical authority[69] vis-à-vis other heads of churches in the communion. Now there was such a need. The definition of the Presiding Bishop as Chief Pastor, and the description of the Episcopal Church as a constituent member of the Anglican Communion, essentially established that (1) by constitution the Episcopal Church considers itself an equal to other provinces in the Anglican Communion, and (2) by canon at least one characteristic of metropolitical authority was recognized as part of the functions of the Presiding Bishop—that of Chief Pastor.

A recommendation of the Lambeth Conference in 1978 led to the first meeting of the primates, or metropolitans, of the Anglican Communion in 1979. In that year Canon 2.4 was changed again to define the duties of the Presiding Bishop as "Chief Pastor and Primate." Again there was a clear relationship between inter-Anglican activities and the redefinition of the Presiding Bishop's duties. In the 1979 General Convention *Journal,* the Presiding Bishop was titled "Most Reverend," and in 1982 the consistent use of that title in the *Episcopal Church Annual* began. With the election of Bishop Edmond Browning in 1985, that honorific became one normally used by the Presiding Bishop himself.

Bishop Neill's niceties of distinction—that the Presiding Bishop is not a metropolitan, and that his title should be The Right Reverend—have been overtaken primarily by changes in the need for inter-Anglican equivalency among leaders of provinces. The Presiding Bishop does not exercise internal metropolitical authority.[70] What is clear is that specific changes in the constitution and in the canons describing duties of the Presiding Bishop have been made to meet international needs of Anglican solidarity. It is an acknowledgment that the concern for hierarchical parity has repercussions in the structural life of specific provinces.

(B) A Case Study of Maps: The Missionary Map of the Anglican Communion

Maps are icons, often of power. There are two world maps of the Anglican Communion now in wide circulation, at least in the United States: the map entitled "The Partner Churches of the Anglican Communion," and the map in the center page of *The Anglican Communion*, a publication of the Anglican Communion Secretariat. These maps are attempts to indicate the *jurisdictional reach* of the Anglican Communion, that is, the areas of the world where bishops of one or another of the churches in the Anglican Communion have some sense of pastoral and administrative responsibility. They reflect, in an iconographic way, the problems within Anglicanism concerning our missionary and ecclesial role in the universal church. They also raise an as yet unanswered question: Is it the intent of the bishops of the Anglican Communion, or of any of the provinces of the communion, to color the world Anglican? That is, is there a missionary hope that, wherever there are "nations and peoples" (using the phrase of the Lambeth Quadrilateral), there will be Anglican churches?

In looking at these maps we should keep several things in mind:

(1) The ancient canonical rule that dioceses and jurisdictions of diocesan bishops should not overlap. In a divided Christendom this rule has been modified to concern dioceses and diocesans of churches in full communion with one another.

(2) The Anglican sense that autonomous churches, provinces, exist in cultural-political frameworks.[71] This gives rise to the *ideal* of a

church for each nation, and the church, no matter how small, being a church *of* the nation.

(3) The continued presence of Anglican churches that primarily support an expatriate community of church members in diaspora. Often called chaplaincies, these churches are often stereotypically under-stood to cater to English and American Anglicans working "overseas." In fact, many of these churches are now supporting Anglicans who come from Anglican churches in the "South."

Concerning overlapping jurisdictions: There are several areas of the world that are colored on the map as having Anglican jurisdictions that are in fact areas of multiple jurisdiction, therefore contrary to the spirit of ancient canon. The primary one is Europe, where there are several rather jarring anomalies. Both the Episcopal Church and the Church of England exercise immediate jurisdiction in Europe as a whole, with the Diocese of Europe and the Convocation of American Churches in Europe. The Convocation, it might be argued, is not a diocese. Nonethe-less, it does have a bishop in charge and a synodical organization with clergy and lay participation, and an annual convention. Additionally, the Diocese of Europe includes ministries in both Portugal and Spain, where there are bishops of jurisdiction for churches now fully integrat-ed into the Anglican family of churches.[72]

The second major jurisdictional anomaly of this sort is in the Philippines, where the comparatively large Philippine Independent Church (over a million members) and the quite small Episcopal Church of the Philippines (less than a hundred thousand members) exist side by side as two churches fully in communion. The Episcopal Church of the Philippines is the direct result of the U.S. Episcopal Church's mis-sionary efforts. Because it was part of the Episcopal Church until 1990, it has belonged to the Anglican Communion from its inception as a mis-sionary district. The Philippine Independent Church has the older his-tory in the Philippines, and its bishops received the historic episcopate in 1948 from the U.S. Episcopal Church.[73] Concordats between each of the Philippine churches and both the Episcopal Church and the Church of England effectively defeat the principle of one bishop or church of jurisdiction in any area.

Concerning national churches: The growth of the communion is often measured in the number of provinces, noted on most maps by different colors, or by borders. There are now over thirty-three jurisdictions. We may have an Anglican Communion by the year 2010 in which there are as many as thirty-five to forty separate provinces.

All of this seems an extension of the long-standing sense in Anglican thought that the church exists within the framework of the people, usually expressed in the context of a nation. While there is no longer any sense in which the Anglican churches are normally the established churches of the nations where they exist, there is a continuing sense in which they can be considered churches *for* these nations. The assumption now seems to be developing that every nation with sufficient Anglican dioceses should be a province, with an archbishop or metropolitan. Like the question of coloring the map Anglican, this assumption has mostly gone unchallenged.[74]

Concerning chaplaincies: A remarkable and often misunderstood ministry is provided by Anglican chaplaincies—Anglican churches that exist to serve expatriates where there is no Anglican mission to the national population. The work of lay and ordained persons in these settings, mostly isolated from other Anglicans and often from other Christians, has often been difficult but magnificent. From one standpoint, therefore, it is with considerable pride that we can say, for example, that the Anglican Communion is present in Libya, by way of a church and congregation in the capital. At the same time, however, it is misleading to color in Libya and all of North Africa on the basis of one chaplaincy in each country. The whole of the Anglican presence in North Africa west of Egypt is to be numbered in the hundreds of persons and exists in only a small handful of churches.

In some places this limited presence needs to be marked with particular care. For example, although the maps would have us believe there is an Anglican jurisdiction in Ethiopia, in fact there is episcopal oversight of one parish in Addis Ababa and an extremely valuable joint project of that parish and the Orthodox Church of Ethiopia for the care of orphans. Furthermore, it is important that we not be seen as claiming jurisdiction in Ethiopia, since Anglicans have affirmed that the Orthodox Church of Ethiopia is in fact the church of the nation, and that there is no need for another church with the historic episcopate. It is something of an embarrassment to have Ethiopia claimed as an

Anglican jurisdiction, a potential insult to the Orthodox and a misrepresentation of our own historical decisions concerning mission.

China presents another awkward case. On the "Partner Churches" map it is labeled "The Holy Catholic Church of China," and all of China is colored in. In *The Anglican Communion* map it is not outlined at all. Which is correct? It is not easy to say. On the one hand, there is the remnant of the historic episcopate in the People's Republic of China, and there is the ongoing remnant of the Chinese church in Hong Kong. But the Anglicans in the PRC have become part of the China Christian Council, which is not committed to anything like Anglican polity. The churches are effectively post-denominational. At least some of what the Lambeth Quadrilateral sets as the context for discussions about reunion has been outdistanced by the experience of the Chinese church. It is to be hoped that we can receive from and extend to the churches in China a real sense of full communion and common purpose, but we ought not claim an Anglican jurisdiction in China.

I suggest that the more accurate map is the one in *The Anglican Communion,* and that correctives to it would make it clear that the Diocese of Egypt has chaplaincies in North African countries and Ethiopia, and that the Chinese Christian Council is clearly not an Anglican jurisdiction. I would also suggest that, until the Anglican Consultative Council can work out an appropriate solution to the problem of Europe, we note the extra-provincial dioceses of the Lustitanian Church and the Reformed Church of Spain, and the presence in European countries, including Spain and Portugal, of chaplaincies of both the Church of England and the Episcopal Church. That is, we would not color *as Anglican* Europe, China, or North Africa and Ethiopia. At least we could keep this small bit of triumphalism under control.

That of course is the issue. Coloring maps is a way to make icons, and such icons are essentially markers of expansionism. What is really being said in making such maps is unfortunately too clear. The maps are announced by title as being about "Partner Churches," or about "the Anglican Communion." But what they say in their iconography is that the world is being colored in—that Anglican churches are spreading across the globe, and that there are more and more Anglican jurisdictions. This is meant to show, along with the estimates of large membership (seventy million), that the Anglican Communion should be taken seriously as a world church.

I am convinced that this is far from the overt intention of any of the mapmakers. Indeed, on one level, Anglican bodies from the Lambeth Conference to the local parish have been wonderfully reluctant to claim more than the fellowship among churches and peoples. But at the same time, it is easy for the expansionist missionary spirit of the past to reappear in the present. In the past the spirit of mission sometimes moved from the humbling effort to bring the good news to the more triumphal desire to dot the landscape with missions and the capitals with bishoprics.

In the present we sometimes move regrettably from a focus on Christ's presence in the world and a desire to restore all persons to unity with God and one another, to the pride of having our own kind spread across the globe. Which is to say, the sin of modern Anglican engagement is the sin of inordinate pride in our own tribe. Coloring the map Anglican can be a statement of thanksgiving for community. It can also be a statement of conquest. In that difference the problem of the future of the Anglican Communion lies. Phrased succinctly: Do we call ourselves the Anglican Communion as an act of thanksgiving for fellowship, or as a claim to power?

SUMMARY

Finding the Anglican Communion involves more than looking at the history of the Anglicanism. It requires that we explore the mutuality and fellowship of churches spread across the world and find in them the received understanding of the practice of church. What joins us together is not an English past, but a sense of community. We remember in our prayers those who in England struggled to establish Anglican sensibilities, and we give thanks for their witness. Those sensibilities are now the basis for the communion's own provisional practice. It is to these sensibilities that we now turn. In the next chapters we will look at the Anglican Communion's understanding of the church, our theological roots in the Incarnation, and our practice of living out the implications of the Incarnation.

ENDNOTES

1. Hill, *The English Bible and the Seventeenth-Century Revolution*, 19.

2. Bosch, *Transforming Mission*, 262.

3. See Paul Avis, "What is 'Anglicanism'?" in Sykes and Booty, *The Study of Anglicanism*, 406–7, for a fine statement of the origins of the word.

4. Chapter 1 of Sykes and Booty, *The Study of Anglicanism*, 3–28.

5. D. Holmes, *A Brief History of the Episcopal Church*, 8.

6. Ibid., 9.

7. "Early Anglican expansion can be conveniently summarized under the not unattractive association of 'Gain and the Gospel.'" Neill, *Anglicanism* (1977), 203.

8. Neill, *A History of Christian Missions*, 194.

9. T. E. Yates, "Anglicans and Mission," in Sykes and Booty, *The Study of Anglicanism*, 430. Yates's essay is a fine summation of the history of Anglican mission.

10. Sykes and Booty, *The Study of Anglicanism*, 210.

11. Turner and Sugeno, *Crossroads Are for Meeting*, 67–90.

12. Ibid., 68.

13. The effects of this conserving effort can still be seen in the remnants of loyalty to the liturgy of the 1662 Book of Common Prayer in some parts of the world. I attended the eucharist at the cathedral in Nairobi in 1989, and not only was that book still in use, the celebration was from the north end of the altar.

14. In some places it was "established" with state support, with rather complicated results.

15. Perry Butler, "From the Early Eighteenth Century to the Present Day," in Sykes and Booty, *The Study of Anglicanism*, 18.

16. The Book of Common Prayer, 877.

17. Rawlinson, *The Anglican Communion in Christendom*, 9.

18. Ibid., 35–36.

19. Ibid., 38.

20. Ibid., 42.

21. Ibid., 44.

22. Ibid., 52.

23. Ibid., 121.

24. Morgan, *Agenda for Anglicans.*

25. Ibid., 10.

26. Ibid., 11.

27. Ibid., 26.

28. Ibid., 77.

29. Ibid., 143.

30. Ibid., 162.

31. Heuss, *The Implications of the Toronto Manifesto*, 3.

32. Ibid.

33. Ibid., 5.

34. Ibid., 6.

35. General Convention, *Annotated Constitution and Canons*, 1:1.

36. Heuss, ibid., 1.

37. Webster, *Mutual Irresponsibility: A Danger to Be Avoided.*

38. Ibid., 15.

39. Ibid., 19.

40. Ibid., 19.

41. See Ian T. Douglas, *Fling Out the Banner*, 288–93, for a detailed account of the rapid expansion and then slow but steady decline in missionary engagement, which was accompanied by the death of the "national church ideal."

42. This is an ongoing discussion, witness the October 1996 meeting of the ACC, in which there was an effort to define the instruments of Anglican unity, viz. the Archbishop of Canterbury, the Lambeth Conference, the Primates' Meetings, and the ACC. Only in the last of these, the ACC, is there any participation of the laity or clergy other than bishops.

43. In Wright, *Quadrilateral at One Hundred*, 156–77.

44. Ibid., 162.

45. Ibid., 177.

46. Ibid., 158.

47. Ibid., 165.

48. Ibid., 177.

49. Paul Avis, *Anglicanism and the Christian Church*, xvii.

50. Ibid., 5.

51. Ibid., 4.

52. Ibid., 5.

53. Ibid., 16.

54. Ibid., 17.

55. Ibid., 20.

56. Ibid., 311.

57. William L. Sachs, *The Transformation of Anglicanism*, 2.

58. Ibid., 74.

59. Ibid., 117.

60. See Douglas, *Fling out the Banner*, 33–38, for an account of the development of the missionary episcopate.

61. This is supported by the phrase, "The Historic Episcopate, locally adapted in the methods of its administration to the varying needs of the nations and peoples called of God into the unity of His Church." The Book of Common Prayer, 877.

62. Sachs, ibid., 122.

63. Ibid., 165. Sachs is the only person I have read who uses the word *confederation*. In this I think he is correct. It is certainly not a federation, though some have called it that.

64. Ibid., 243–44.

65. Ibid., 336.

66. Taped statement from video directed by James L. Friedrich, *The Story of Anglicanism* (Los Angeles: Cathedral Films and Video), part 3.

67. Neill, *Anglicanism* (1963), 286–87.

68. Ibid., 286, n. 1.

69. By "metropolitical authority" is meant authority exercised by a bishop, usually set apart as "archbishop," over other bishops and their jurisdictions.

The organizational grouping of dioceses and their bishops constitutes a province, usually meeting in synod, over which the Metropolitan exercises authority. The matter is complicated because in the Church of England, where the Archbishop of Canterbury is Metropolitan and Primate of All England, the Archbishop of York also exercises metropolitical authority and is called Primate of England. The Episcopal Church has domestic provinces as well. The presidents of such provinces do not exercise metropolitical authority. However, the question here is what authority the Presiding Bishop has in the Episcopal Church, equivalent to the metropolitical authority exercised in other provinces of the Anglican Communion.

70. Certain changes were passed at the 1997 General Convention that would further limit the authority and work of the Presiding Bishop. It is unclear just what these might mean vis-à-vis his authority as metropolitan within the Episcopal Church.

71. An example of the thinking of the ACC on the matter is this: "A province must have some common constitution, its geographical and political area must allow good communications, and however much it transcends linguistic, national, or cultural boundaries, its peoples must have a community of concern which can unite them in a community of worship." ACC, *The Time is Now*, 35.

72. I am happy to say that work is now under way to correct this anomaly.

73. Neill, *Anglicanism*, 4th ed., 374.

74. It is certainly alluded to in *Anglicanism and the Universal Church*, 57–58, where John Howe speaks, in some despair, of areas where "the spread of Anglicanism is thin."

CHAPTER 2

AN ANGLICAN COMMUNION UNDERSTANDING OF THE CHURCH

A COMMUNITY OF MUTUALITY

To envision our future as Anglicans we must first ask what we have already envisioned as our work, our mission. Anglicans believe themselves to be part of the ongoing universal Christian church; thus, the mission we examine is not that of Anglicans alone, but is related to the mission of the whole church.

The Book of Common Prayer of the Episcopal Church says in its catechism, "The mission of the Church is to restore all people to unity with God and each other in Christ."[1] It is, of course, quite out of the question that the "church" understood as any of the organizations we know of should accomplish this. The church is not, in this "mission statement," an agency of human making. Rather, it is the instrument of God's will and compassion. That is why speaking of the mission of the church is really one way of speaking of God's mission, in the context of which the church has its function. It is important to distinguish "church" in this sense from the organizations we know and can analyze as social phenomena. Churches, including the Anglican churches, are such social entities, but church—as the agency of God's Mission—is quite another thing.

Anglican theologians mostly agree that the peculiar Anglican experience in responding to the mission of the church is not to be confused with the experience of the whole church. That is, we do not claim to have a universal understanding or experience of the mission of the church. Rather, we have our experiences, and these are available to and part of the wider understanding of the mission of the church. In this chapter we will look at several aspects of the Anglican experience of mission. This in turn will tell us something about what it is we bring, in the Anglican Communion, to the wider church and the total mission of God.

KOINONIA

The writer of Acts reports that the followers of Jesus were first called "Christians" in Antioch (Acts 11:26). We can be fairly sure that disagreements about what this designation meant and about what was essential to Christian life were there from the beginning. Still, for most persons in the early church, at least two sacramental events were experienced and agreed on as essential: baptism and communion. These sacraments assumed a gathered community, a congregation, and a sense of partnership and fellowship.

The word in Greek for the gathered community of the church, as for a meeting, is most often *ekklesia*, and for the community as a gathered in fellowship, it is *koinonia*. In Anglican thought *koinonia* is a word that carries great weight and is often used to describe what we are about. We are, it is said, a *koinonia*. We are not alone in our attachment to that word, but it has become something of a touchstone for Anglicans.

Koinonia is a word with a variety of meanings in Greek, many of which are important to its flavor, even as used by Anglicans with little Greek language ability. These meanings are proper to the Greek word but largely lost when the word is translated as "fellowship." Gerhard Kittel's *Theological Dictionary of the New Testament* and John Koenig's *New Testament Hospitality* provide ways of appreciating the wider sense of the word and what it would have suggested to the New Testament community that referred to itself as a *koinonia*. Much of what follows is based on Koenig's insights in *New Testament Hospitality*, though without doing his work justice.

The Greek *koinonia* is usually translated "fellowship" or "participation," but with a wide range of variations depending on the context and social location of the word's use.[2] It can mean sharing between two people; sharing in a common enterprise; imparting to someone; a legal partnership. In the stem *koinon-* is the idea of the common share in a thing; the sharing of all with all, as in a cosmic harmony; or the sharing at table, particularly at table with the gods. This last possibility— sharing at table with the gods—presented a real problem for Jews or Christians who might use the word.

In the New Testament, the religious fellowship found uniquely in the table-sharing of the eucharist—the sharing of membership in the Body of Christ—raises participation and fellowship to a level where use of the word needed to be carefully circumscribed. If the Greeks understood *koinonia* to mean, on occasion, fellowship with the gods, how could it be used by Jewish Christians who, while wanting to build on the image of fellowship in Christ, would abhor the idea of a friendly and intimate relationship with the Most High God?

Paul found an answer in two special applications of the word koinonia. The first was its use to name a spiritual fellowship. In the community's sharing in the life, death, and resurrection of Christ, *koinonia* took on a special meaning. The Christian community shared in the whole redemptive presence of Christ, and the word implied a mutuality not only among the members (a fellowship of believers), but also between believers and the Christ (a fellowship in the Body), and between believers and Christ together with the Holy Spirit (a fellowship of participation in the Spirit). Thus, *koinonia* came to mean the communion of the shared meal itself and the totality of participation in the mutuality available in the community. In this way, the mutuality of all in the koinonia of the Christian community yielded a "fellowship of brotherly concord established and expressed in the life of the community."[3] This differs from the wider Greek use of *koinonia* in that it stops short of direct fellowship with the Creator. Kittel understands Paul's use to conform to the church's general attitude that the way to the Father is through the Son, and that fellowship with Christ is fellowship with God.

The second stress in Paul's use of *koinonia* concerned partnerships between people, particularly economic and hospitality partnerships. John Koenig's investigation of this understanding of *koinonia* is particularly helpful for Anglicans, because it takes the vertical dimension of the fellowship—between God and humankind—and opens it out horizontally to the fellowship of believers as we go about the business of everyday life.[4]

Writers on Anglican Communion perspectives are given to talking about *koinonia* and equating it with fellowship, or when a spiritual fellowship, with communion. The problem, of course, is that fellowship is a broadly available word, used for life in a club ("come join our fellowship, you'll really like the bowling"), life in a political organization (I once belonged to a group called the Woodsworth-Irving Socialist Fellowship), or even a sinister group ("his integration into the fellowship of the Knights of the Ku Klux Klan was complete when he joined them in a cross burning"). So the word *fellowship* is not really adequate. Christians who use this term mean a special sort of fellowship.

Taking the clue from *communion,* which is in some ways almost too narrow a definition of fellowship, we can at least say that *koinonia* means a particular kind of fellowship. It is one in which the mutuality can include, and is understood to make possible, the sharing of the sacred meal, communion with Jesus, and partnership with one another in Christ. I would suggest then that koinonia be understood as "community of mutuality" in which sharing is based on the paradigm of the sharing of the eucharistic meal. The elements of *mutuality*—a sharing of one's self and the resources of fellowship—and *community*—a fellowship not of convenience or occasion, but of unity (communion)—are combined in the one word.[5]

THE MARKS OF ANGLICAN KOINONIA

The word *koinonia* is what is understood to lie behind the word *fellowship* as used in the constitution of the Episcopal Church when it defines the Anglican Communion:

The Episcopal Church. . .is a constituent member of the
Anglican Communion, a Fellowship within the One, Holy,
Catholic, and Apostolic Church, of those duly constituted
Dioceses, Provinces, and regional Churches in communion
with the See of Canterbury, upholding and propagating the
historic Faith and Order as set forth in the Book of Common
Prayer.[6]

By this definition the Anglican Communion is a fellowship, but one
of a particular sort, marked by several characteristics. The constitution
describes these as follows:

(1) It is within the *One, Holy, Catholic, and Apostolic Church*;

(2) it consists of groups of Christians (dioceses, provinces, and
regional churches) *in communion with the See of Canterbury*;

(3) it upholds and propagates "the historic *Faith and Order*"; and

(4) it defines faith and order "as set forth *in the Book of Common
Prayer.*"

In some ways this is a wonderfully clear definition of the Anglican
Communion, put together by a church so often accused of being unruly
and muddled. Each of these elements has been greatly stretched and
tested by the actual experience of the church over the years. Even a
brief look will give us some sense of the breadth of issues we face in
trying to envision a vocation in which the notion of a community of
mutuality is central.

We have a basic sense of the Anglican Communion as related to
what the earliest church was about: incorporation into the body of
believers and table fellowship. In this sense, the Anglican Communion
participates in the life of primitive Christianity, the "church before
there was church." But the constitutional definition quickly turns to the
ways in which church was formed by its communal experience and
identifies itself more formally and institutionally. It is a fellowship, but
one whose character involves a *mutuality*. It takes its meaning from the
sense of being a collective of dioceses within the church as the Body of
Christ.

(1) ONE, HOLY, CATHOLIC, AND APOSTOLIC

The definition of the Anglican Communion as a fellowship in the
One, Holy, Catholic, and Apostolic Church draws on what Peter C.

Hodgson calls "Elements of the Church in the Classic Paradigm."[7] According to Hodgson, The New Testament provided the classic images of the church as:

(a) the *People of God*;

(b) the *Body of Christ* (on three levels, as crucified Christ, risen Christ, and cosmic Christ);

(c) the *Communion of faith, hope and love*;

(d) the *Creation of the Spirit*.

These images were always subject to the core understanding of the proclamation and manifestation of the Kingdom of God, known in Jesus Christ. In the face of that proclamation and manifestation, the church in history is always "fragmentary and ambiguous,"[8] falling short of the paradigm and vision.

One of the first formulations of a coherent ecclesiology based on these images—that of the church as one, holy, catholic, and apostolic—was so powerful that it became incorporated in the creed of Nicea-Constantinople, and it was so enduring that it is integral to the preface to the constitution of the Episcopal Church, written some eighteen hundred years later. John Howe and others have called the elements of this credal formulation the "marks of the Church."

> The Anglican Church thinks in terms of one continuing Church—one, holy, catholic and apostolic. Those "four marks of the Church" derive through the creeds, and are often used in Anglicanism. They are a better description than the name "Anglicanism" because Anglicans think in terms of one continuing and universal Church.[9]

The four marks are held by Hodgson to limit the imagery behind the credal formula because of their specific roles in determining orthodox coherence. He sees them as marks of continuing value, but only if freed from the narrow definitions imposed by a rationalist scheme of propositions. With this proviso, they remain determinative for Anglicans.

It is important to note that these marks of Christian fellowship are criticized in some quarters because they seem to limit the church's experience to the service of theological and ecclesial needs of the period from the third to the eighteenth century. These marks were developed in their full credal sense *during the period when the church was*

modeled on the empire. We must always remember that what we understand as wonderfully coherent and eminently sensible is sometimes
seen by others as dogmatic and authoritarian. Where we hear the words
"one," "holy," "catholic," and "apostolic" and understand them collectively to be a sign of unity in our Lord, others equally committed to
Jesus Christ see them as limits on truth-seeking, limits imposed by
imperialistically minded western authoritarians. For example, people
might find the word "apostolic" less than useful in their thinking about
the faith if that word has carried the weight of historical patriarchy, as
in the title "Apostolic Nuncio" or the doctrine of "Apostolic Succession." For some, the weight of such titles and doctrines has been used
to crush belief and thought. Thus, while this mark of Anglican *koinonia* describes our understanding of who we are, it is not necessarily good
news to some of our Christian neighbors, whose ancestors suffered persecution by our ancestors.

(2) COMMUNION WITH THE SEE OF CANTERBURY

Fellowship, particularly as we have defined it here, involves both
individuals and communities. The core model is, however, personal.
Christian fellowship, *koinonia,* involves communion—table fellowship.
The Anglican Communion is understood to be a fellowship of *churches*;
but because the model is personal, the personal witness of those repre-
senting the various churches determines whether those churches are in
Anglican fellowship. Breaking bread becomes the sacramental basis
for saying we are in communion with one another as churches. In particular, for the Anglican Communion, the fellowship of our churches
has come to mean that our bishops are *personally* in communion with
the *person* of the Archbishop of Canterbury, who in his *person* represents the See of Canterbury.

This has placed an extraordinary burden on the Archbishop of
Canterbury. Along with his role as bishop of a diocese, metropolitan of
the church, and state officer, he has also become in his person the focal
point for Anglican unity. Historically it is quite understandable that
this has happened. And to the great credit of the persons holding the
office of Archbishop, this burden has been borne with grace.

There is some power in this role, and it is, interestingly, power that
begins from the simple table-fellowship issue: inviting others to share

the meal. The decision of whom to invite to the Lambeth Conference, whether to call a meeting of the primates,[10] or who is to be Secretary General of the Anglican Consultative Council (ACC), rests either directly or indirectly with the Archbishop of Canterbury. That invitation, calling, or nomination can in turn have immense implications for the credibility of those invited. If one of the identifying marks of being part of the Anglican Communion is communion with the See of Canterbury, and if that is important to a diocese or national church, for reasons as often social and political as spiritual, the invitation from the Archbishop to the Lambeth Conference is crucial.

In several instances in recent years, being invited to the Lambeth Conference has mattered a great deal. For several years beginning in 1986, the Episcopal Church of the Sudan had two persons claiming to be Archbishop. Each had bishops loyal to him and his synod; each had difficult relations with the national government and the liberation movement, in the context of civil war. Knowing who represented the congregations of this several-million-member church was a matter of great importance. A great effort was made to resolve this situation, but without much success. Finally, who was Archbishop in the Sudan was determined by the litmus test of seeing who would receive the invitation from the Archbishop of Canterbury to attend the Lambeth Conference and whom the Archbishop of Canterbury would visit when he went to the Sudan. When he decided, the matter was effectively closed.[11]

In the debate and division within several provinces of the Anglican Communion over the ordination of women, small groups of dissenters have formed new dioceses and national or regional churches. Some of these churches have appealed to the Archbishop of Canterbury for recognition as part of the Anglican family of churches. Such recognition has been withheld.

The Archbishop's refusal to be in communion with these bodies has been a confirmation for churches like the Anglican Church of Canada and the Episcopal Church in the U.S. that their processes, even if they lead to what seems to be fairly radical reform, are nonetheless processes that are honored by the communion as a whole. The Archbishop of Canterbury has not acted alone in this, of course, but his actions are finally his own, in the sense that all opinions he elicits are, strictly speaking, advice only.[12]

Certain groups of dissenters have continued as members in the churches from which they came, but are attempting to develop non-territorial jurisdictions. These have not been yet recognized by the provincial leaders meeting together, in part for political considerations, in part because of the ancient canon that prohibits more than one bishop from having primary jurisdiction in the same territory. The whole matter has become muddled, however, by recent actions of the Church of England that have essentially allowed for extra-territorial pastoral oversight of parishes that do not wish to have women clergy. Where this will go is unclear, but the rubric of pastoral sensitivity effectively encourages dissenting groups in the United States and elsewhere to claim extra-territorial status within the structures of regional autonomous Anglican provinces.[13]

It would seem this characteristic mark of the Anglican Communion is rather straightforward and uncomplicated, but there are several points of difficulty. First, this mark of communion involves power and authority flowing in only one direction—from all the other dioceses, bishops and primates *to the Archbishop of Canterbury*. It concerns table-fellowship *at his invitation*. Conversations have already been had, and will continue to be had, concerning models of communion that have greater mutuality.

Second, the See of Canterbury is honored for historical reasons. Leadership in the communion is focused on the incumbent of Canterbury because of his status as the primate of the "mother church." The two factors of honor and leadership are woven together in several ways.

For many years the term *first among equals* has been used to describe the relationship between the Archbishop of Canterbury and the bishops of the Anglican Communion. This has meant that he is held in special regard by the communion. His sponsorship of the Lambeth Conferences and his care for the unity of the communion are acknowledged as pastoral offices of the highest value. But "first among equals" has been a title of appreciation more than one of authority, although it is clearly a heartfelt description.

Beginning with the 1954 Minneapolis Anglican Congress the Archbishop's duties have expanded considerably. The formation of the ACC in 1969 and the regular meetings of the primates beginning in

1979 required that the Archbishop take on new duties. He is now expected to relate to a variety of ongoing instruments of Anglican unity because of the symbolic first-among-equals status of his office. He holds no appointed or elected office whereby he may preside over any meeting other than ones he calls. It is the symbolic value of the office of Archbishop of Canterbury that gives him mandate.

In the report of the meeting of the ACC and the primates held in 1993, titled "A Transforming Vision," the Archbishop of Canterbury signed himself "George Cantuar, Primus inter pares [First Among Equals]," and the caption under a sketched picture of him used the title "Primus inter pares" as well.[14] Some, myself included, are concerned that this signifies the beginning of a more formal assertion that the Archbishop of Canterbury is indeed *by primacy of place* invested with power. It opens the issue of whether he is becoming de facto the Patriarch of the Anglican Communion. Again, the drift is a subtle one, and it is traceable, I believe, to a trend in the communion which fosters dreams of being a world church, a kingdom like other kingdoms, with its own real patriarch.

If the Anglican Communion is to be a world church, it will be useful to discuss the form of leadership we might expect. The discussion should consider some process for appointment or election of the patriarch, the funding of the "international headquarters," the decision-making authority of its governing councils, and the ability to tax member churches.

If, on the other hand, the definition prevails that the Anglican Communion is a "Fellowship within the One, Holy, Catholic, and Apostolic Church," there is no justification for a patriarchate and no structure inherent in the development of the network of that fellowship's members that requires power to be located or focused in one place only.

My sense is that neither *koinonia* nor Anglican sensibilities are served well by patriarchal drift. The unfortunate result of such drift would be greater hierarchical dependency and (perhaps) greater use of authority as the basis for establishing and maintaining correct belief. There are those who would argue that this whole matter is of little significance. But I would contend that how we honor those who lead says something about what we think we need in leaders.

In the first century, Peter was honored in community, but rather quickly that honor was transferred to his chair, which was in a particular place; so now his chair is honored, and by extension, the one who occupies it. The question in the Anglican Communion is what it means to honor the chair of Augustine of Canterbury. Are we by this honor giving primacy to the one who sits on that chair as our patriarch or matriarch, and are we envisioning a hierarchical rather than conciliar church? And if we do so, what will become of our sense of *koinonia*?

(3) HISTORIC FAITH AND ORDER

This mark of the Anglican Communion concerns reformation ideals and ecumenical hopes: Our faith is *historic* because, as the Reformation thinkers contended, it is necessary to reform by returning again and again to the witness of the earliest universal church, known immediately in scripture and less directly in antiquity or tradition. The sign of universality is again communion—writ large in the contexts in which bishops gather in council, but also known to the people in common prayer and sacrament. The notion of a historic faith builds on what we have learned in community about our faith and becomes expressed in our common prayer, in scripture as the primary informing source, and in certain instruments of our common council—the creeds in particular.

The matter of *order*, however, relies on other characteristics of communion. We must discern the forms of ministry needed and the forms of order in our common life of worship. The disarray of four hundred years of Protestant fragmentation and of almost one thousand years since the split of the eastern and western churches cries out for a renewed sense of common order. The phrase "Faith and Order" became the rallying cry around which the ecumenical movement of the twentieth century was formed, and when that is combined with the word "historic" we see the full import of this mark of the Anglican Communion. [15]

The Anglican Communion is marked by a reliance on scripture, the faith of the church as developed in council, and the sacramental ordering of common life. There is an echo in this of the Lambeth Quadrilateral, of which more will be said at a later point. The notion of historic faith and order does not necessarily imply the episcopate as we have come to know it, but it does imply an ordered communal life. Most of what constitutes faith and order builds on, but is not identical to, the experience recorded in scripture. The usual formula, that "Holy Scripture containeth all things necessary to salvation: so that whatsoever is not read therein, nor may be proved thereby, is not to be required of any man, that it should be believed as an article of the Faith, or be thought requisite or necessary to salvation,"[16] raises the question of the historic justification of most matters of order, and some of faith.

Can we, for example, deduce anything of certainty about the order of priests from the New Testament "order" of elders? Can the wording of the creeds be proved by scripture? "Historic Faith and Order" is not a simple mechanism for returning to the "primitive" church, a task which is in any event impossible, but rather an appeal to sensibilities congruent with those held by the majority of Christians in the first three centuries. We cannot be totally consistent with the early church; too much of the physical and mental furniture has been moved about. But perhaps we can be focused on the same Person as they, and in ways they would have recognized as faithful.

(4) THE BOOK OF COMMON PRAYER

Without question, one of the best-known peculiarities and characteristics of Anglicanism is our use of the Book of Common Prayer. In the Episcopal Church, we are all aware of changes in our book. Because most Anglicans live in one Province and use one book, we are often less aware that changes are happening in other parts of the communion—changes sometimes quite distinct from those taking place in our own church. It is not, then, our current book, or even the collection of current books, per se, that constitute this mark. Rather is the *historic* connection of whatever book is now in use (with or without that title), and the English Book of Common Prayer of 1662 and its predecessors, and a *faithfulness* to a Prayer Book sensibility, that are the mark. We are identified not by the common use, worldwide, of a single book, but by our common inheritance of the one Book of Common Prayer used by the English for almost the whole period of its missionary expansion.

Of course that, too, does not exhaust the matter. Inheritance is only as much as one makes of it, and there is some evidence that, in dioceses where the English liturgy is a reminder of colonial repression or where the English language is irrelevant, there may be only minimal interest in the source of Anglican liturgy in the 1662 Church of England Prayer Book, and even less in its predecessors. One may well ask if there is any reason to continue to insist that the unity rests on the Book of Common Prayer at all. Perhaps a better understanding is that we share a religious sensibility in which there is a common rule of prayer. At least that affirms our indebtedness to our monastic heritage.

Each of these characteristic marks of the Anglican Communion appears on the surface to be relatively straightforward. But in each there are provisos: We are "One, Holy, Catholic, and Apostolic," provided that these do not become calls to imperial thoughts. We are in communion with the See of Canterbury, provided that this does not require acquiescence to "foreign" authority. We uphold and propagate the historic faith and order, provided that we know faith and order are more a matter of focus than a matter of doctrinal or structural life. We define our faith and order "as set forth" in the Book of Common Prayer, provided that it is understood that faith and order come from the common life of prayer, not this or that prayer book.

We have these marks, but they are provisionally held. That provisionality is itself a characteristic of our common life.

PROVISIONALITY OF STRUCTURE AND THEOLOGICAL DOCTRINE

The Anglican experience of community, *koinonia*, may be understood by first looking at outward signs or marks of fellowship. But along with that exterior experience there is also an inner experience of many Anglican thinkers from the Reformation to the present. One of the primary experiences has been that of provisionality, the sense that all that we have as doctrine is provisionally stated, and awaits the full disclosure of God for completion. This is echoed in the Reformation words of the preface to the first Book of Common Prayer (1549): "There was never any thing by the wit of man so well devised, or so sure established, which in continuance of time hath not been corrupted. . .";[17] and in the careful balancing act of the Articles of Religion: "As the Church of Jerusalem, Alexandria and Antioch, have erred; so also the

Church of Rome have erred. . ."[18] (and by implication, so have the Church of England and others). Thus there is always a need to accept provisionally what is decided in the councils of the church.

I want to recount a reverie that I had in October 1994. It was a very distinct and well-ordered dream, which I remember clearly. I remember, too, that immediately afterwards I knew it to be a beginning point for an argument for the importance of provisional thinking in theology.

I dream that I am in this large house, and I go from room to room looking for someone who I know is just ahead of me, leaving each room just before I enter. Sometimes the clues of this person's presence are straightforward: here a rocking chair is still rocking gently; here a fresh ring of wine sits where a glass had been put down and taken up; there I smell remnants of perfume; once I see a door close, and the back of a head, just as I enter the room from another door. I never see the person, but I know there is one.

In the dream I lie down and think about what I might do when I finally meet the one who has preceded me. So I think about the one who has gone before, and I visualize that person present with me. I finally catch up with that person, in a dream within the dream. Then the room where we meet becomes my room, and I meet Jesus.

Sometimes when I am awake I hope for the same thing, that I will finally meet the person Jesus. But here, awake, the matter is not so simple. My visualization is inadequate to the reality of the world. I know there is a difference between the Jesus of my dream and the Jesus of God, who is real. So, awake, I wait.

I imagine that something like this is the state of all Christians. In every age and time, in every moment of joy or terror, of exaltation or degradation, of wasted time or sublime moment, we are brought up short: the Jesus of our dream is not the fullness of the Jesus of God. We dream too small, and we think too culturally bound, to have it any other way. But we await the experience of Jesus as the Jesus of God. Some blessed few have been introduced to the Jesus of God. But most, among them even the most faithful, have not. Rather, we have met only the Jesus of our culture, our hopes, and our times.

T. S. Eliot says, "Human kind cannot bear very much reality."[19] The church exists to bear for us the unbearable press of reality. We must hold in tension our current dream of Jesus and the reality of the Jesus of God. We can barely live with the image of Jesus, we cannot bear the fullness of the Incarnation, the Jesus of God. So the church is always about the tasks of providing us ways to have appropriate images of that which is unimaginable, but finally to be experienced. That task is difficult at best, and the church is tempted to stress the appropriateness of the images it proposes. Churches, therefore, are always open to criticism for giving their images the authority due finally only to the reality of the Jesus of God.

The continual state of affairs in the church is this: It is expected to provide the images for our encounter with Jesus, so that we might experience, even in the unbearable tension of our situation, something of the Jesus of God. This it tries to do through liturgy, theology, dogmatics, pastoral engagement, mystical experience described, evangelism, preaching, ministry, and mission. The problem is that it cannot really meet those expectations. Thus, the church's activities are to be seen always in relation to the level of our disappointment with its ability to do what finally seems impossible: to meet the Jesus of God rather than the Jesus of our expectations.

The Jesus of God—the presence of God with us—is finally realized as an end, and therefore in our present context is an *ideal.* All our visualizations of Jesus are provisional. The Jesus of history is real, but very little is known as *fact* about him. The Jesus of the *church* and of the *faithful* is as provisional as the dream, as solid as a guiding vision, as demanding as any experientially engaged person, but finally a socially determined reality. These meetings, these Jesus experiences, are of invaluable import. But these many experiences are not the Jesus of God. They give us hope that the Jesus of God, who we know is the reality of the Incarnation, will be known to us also in experience. The Jesus of God is known in the church and by individuals through the Holy Spirit, but the Jesus of God is not the same as the Jesus of the church or of the individual. The Holy Spirit informs the church and individuals of the Jesus of God, but our senses and sensibilities always limit the form the witness takes.

What are these experiences then? Perhaps these meetings are the many-layered dream and vision of God incarnate, built up in the church and the memory of faithful people, constituting the fabric of our faith. The hope of Christians is that the dream and the vision are God's way of giving us about as much reality as we can bear.

Therefore, the church needs always to be clear about two things:

(1) Its Jesus is a product of its dreams and visions, God's way of giving us a provisional understanding, sufficient to be borne, as to what God is like in the flesh. This must apply to the best Jesus given in modern scholarship, the simplest Jesus of the Sunday school, the most fiery Jesus of the revolutionary, the quietest Jesus in the heart at prayer. *It is all a gift, and it is all provisional.*

(2) This provisional character of encounter makes all specifically Christian theology provisional, and all authority for doctrine limited. It is to the Jesus of God that judgment and final authority belongs. What the church can say is that it believes its dreams and visions, its histories and presentation of the Jesus in history and of history are God-inspired. But because the church's belief comes from the same place its dreams come from, its belief is no charter for authority.

Because churches are so tempted to claim their beliefs as the truth, and to claim authority on the basis of access to the Jesus of God, and because we have all relied upon the church to provide the appropriate visualization of Jesus, the church finds itself at various times *in a crisis related to authority.* We are in such a period now.

THE CRISIS OF AUTHORITY AND THE NEED FOR PROVISIONALITY

The church has developed a corporate model whose concerns are for institutional stability, and assumes that coherence of its doctrines will further that stability by providing the believer with unwavering values. The crisis that develops is that the coherence of those doctrines and the stability of those values depends on precisely what the church can never show: that its dreams and visions are more than provisional.

The church has provided images of Jesus that support the privatization of belief, and images of its instrumentalities—the clergy, the sacraments, the bible—that make such belief dependent on corporate interpretation. In turn, that corporate interpretation has taken the New

Testament image of the Body of Christ and anthropomorphized it, making some members (the clergy and hierarchy) the "head" and the laity, the people, lesser parts.[20] The church, in other words, has taken the image of incorporation (becoming part of the body) and transformed it into the image of the corporation (taking a specific role in the body). What had been primarily an image about being in the body, and about taking roles in that body as a consequence, become an image about the role of particular participants, and less about being in union in the body.

The history of the development of the corporate nature of the church is the history of the church's reflections on this image of itself as body. As these images became recurrent, with established forms, the churches (now plural) took on specific doctrinal character, and modeled their authority for the surety of these doctrines on the best corporate models at hand. So we have the imperial Church of Rome, the monarchical Church of England, the Swiss Canton model of the Presbyterians, etc., and thus, too, the modern corporate models of many denominations in America. It is difficult to think that Jesus had this in mind when he said, "In my Father's house there are many rooms" (John 14:2).

The crisis of the moment is bound to the end of the modern period of history, in which certain predominant ideas of mostly European origins have been found wanting. The questioning of these ideas has thrown the whole society, and the church along with it, into crisis. The crisis is one of ideas, and is mostly debated by the circles near the sources of authority, but all people feel its effects. These ideas have determined what counts as truth, and therefore of what counts as valid visualizations or idealizations not only of Jesus and the church, but of all important mental constructs.

Principal among these has been the notion of the *subjective* and the notion of available absolute, and therefore true, statements that in turn are about *objective* matters of fact. Beliefs are subjective; knowledge is objective. Belief and faith are paired, as are knowledge and reality. A link between belief and knowledge, faith and reality, was forged in the notion of revealed religion. Statements concerning beliefs are valid, it is argued, if they conform to doctrine; and doctrines are valid as they in turn conform to the authoritative interpretation of the dreams and visions of the several approved sources (the Bible, the Fathers, etc.). The religious insistence has been that revelation is a product of authoritative interpretation. Now, all that is being questioned. Similar questioning is taking place in the sciences, where the notions of a scientific method and pure science are under attack.[21]

Of course such questioning causes camps to develop: Those invested in the hierarchical determination of which dreams and visions will be accepted in the church see the dark cloud of confusion looming. So do many faithful people, who just want a relatively stable vision of Jesus. Those who would dream differently, or who believe the hierarchical determination is invalid, look for alternate ways to provide dreams and visions of the Jesus of God and of the reign he announced.

So the crisis is at its core a crisis of paradigm shift, and its effects are a crisis in authority. There are a wide range of reactions to the dismantling of the core doctrine of revealed truth and the similar scientifically naive notion of scientific truth. The pairing of these two disillusionments—religious and scientific authority—arises at just the time when there is widespread questioning of the effect of such authority in practice. In practice, authority in the modern age has assumed the priority of what it determines as objective truth and in various ways has relegated subjective experience to inferior status. Since the authorities are mostly of white, male, European background, and—in the case of the church—mostly clerics, it is not surprising that religion and science have come to reflect the experience of these men.

This crisis of authority is at the core of the church's problems surrounding the end of modernity. The period from the Enlightenment to the present has mostly assumed that scientific investigation could lead us to knowledge unimpeded by the matrix of social experience in which the investigators practiced. It assumed that religious truths were grounded in authoritative revelation, rather than the matrix of social experience. Both assumptions were, in their practical extension, mistaken, and humans have paid a high price for the error.

There are many groups working out the problem of where to go from here. The crises brought on by the end of modernity lead to a wide range of new ways of thinking. There is the attempt to look with fresh eyes on what was seen as a mechanical universe. Perhaps the universe is in some sense organic, alive. There is also the attempt to see, in a more holistic sense, the truth of the Incarnation, the personal presence in creation of the Creator.[22]

Provisionality is an answer to the press for coherence, and a *counterpoint* to investment in authority as a source of revealed truth. It has also been a strong element of Anglican practice and is seen principally in the Anglican attraction to the image of the *primitive catholic faith*. That image is of the church in the first few centuries, when all of Christianity in council and communion was capable of being a community of mutuality. It is of course only an image. There is every reason to believe that the ideal of mutuality was never realized. Still, primitive communalism was a hope and was sometimes realized (Acts 2:44), and a form of conciliar decision-making was successfully invoked for a time (Acts 15). Appeal to this image is made often enough in discussions of Anglicanism to suggest that it is a central matter for self-understanding. As Anglicans, we understand our faith and life to be an extension of that community of mutuality that produced statements of faith, formed the scripture, and normalized the sacramental life of the community.

Anglican practice also has as one of its distinguishing characteristics the search for comprehensiveness. That search, like the attraction to the primitive catholic faith, is related to the ideal of the universal community of mutuality, and is thought of sometimes as a practical way to emulate what is no longer possible—the conciliar mutuality of the early church. No matter that there may not have been any such ideal period in the life of the Christian community, the search for comprehensiveness has been an ongoing quest in Anglican thought.

KOINONIA GROUNDED IN THE SACRAMENTAL LIFE: ANGLICAN PRACTICE AS THE UNIVERSAL CHURCH IN LOCATION

Anglican religious sensibilities always return to the idea of *common prayer* and *communion*. Both of those are highly localized in their practice. And here the Anglican model is the local parish church. What the Book of Common Prayer did initially was to ensure that "all the realm shall have but one use";[23] that is, it ensured that local practice was joined to that of the whole people. The village church belongs to the whole nation just as the individual, the village, and the nation are all part of the Body of Christ. So we might think of Anglican churches and the Anglican Communion as structures whose purpose is to give support to local houses (communities), to fellowships of mutuality whose mutuality is based in local community and understood as part of the whole. We can look at the Anglican Communion and see it simply as a device reflecting, and supporting, life in community. According to this way of thinking, a church of the Anglican Communion is not something we belong to; rather, it is an instrument for seeing ourselves and the community in which we worship as part of the greater whole, a whole so much greater that even the communion itself is only a hint of it. Following on this, while we might say (and we often do), "I belong to the Episcopal Church," or, "She is a member of the Church of England," we would also insist that we *really* belong to the "church universal," or more popularly, "the catholic church." Belonging to the Episcopal Church, the Church of England, or the Church of Uganda is just our way of going about that.

A GENIUS OF ANGLICANISM REVISITED

In the Anglican community, we seem always to return to the question of polity—to the questions of the basis and order of common life in the faith. This in itself suggests the closeness of our concerns to those of religious orders. Clearly there is a complex interrelation between the formation of the English people, the development of English government, and the spread of Christian faith in England. It is far beyond the scope of this work to look at these complexities. It is sure, however, that somewhere in that forging process, when the notion of a people of a common weal was hammered out, a sensibility about polity arose in which the elements of practice addressed in the previous chapters of this book arose. These elements can be outlined as follows:

(1) Through the churches of which they are a part, Anglicans are members of a fellowship, a *koinonia*, reflected in the Anglican Communion.

(2) There is a mutual affection in that fellowship and an acknowledgment of some commonly held characteristics of that fellowship,

"marks," among which are: being part of the one, holy, catholic, and apostolic church; being in communion with the See of Canterbury; and holding the historic faith and order as set forth in the Book of Common Prayer.

(3) Anglicans are a provisional people, knowing that what we express is for the time being, and that the commitment to the Body of Christ is a commitment to our own end, both as individuals and as a separate church. We have the sense that our fellowship is incomplete, and our faith limited, because of divisions in the Christian community and the obstinacy of opinion made dogma.

(4) Anglican practice begins in the sacramental life as the means of participation in God. This practice is the outward and visible sign of *koinonia*. An Anglican understanding of the practice of church is therefore not limited to the practice of particular Anglican churches, individually or collectively. It is open and porous, willing to work toward that which it cannot yet be, toward a church whose sacramental life is increasingly that of the Body of Christ.

ENDNOTES

1. The Book of Common Prayer, 855.

2. Kittel, *Theological Dictionary of the New Testament*, s.v. *koinonia*.

3. Ibid.

4. See Koenig, *New Testament Hospitality*, chap. 3.

5. *Koinonia* is also a term widely used in ecumenical conversations and has had renewed use in Anglican circles, particularly in the context of the 1988 Lambeth Conference, where it was invoked in discussions of the division over the ordination of women to the episcopate. *Koinonia* denotes a concept of unity that sometimes avoids, *for the benefit of those divided by deeply held theological positions*, the need to assemble as one in *ekklesia*. It is thought possible to have a deeply felt engagement with "fellow" Christians even while we may not sit at table with them. I am arguing here for a stronger sense of *koinonia*, which would presume a mutuality such that gathering as the assembly would be required or anticipated. It would seem that on occasion *koinonia* has been used not to affirm mutuality, but good manners in the face of intractable differences.

6. Preamble to the constitution of the Episcopal Church (General Convention, *Annotated Constitution and Canons,* 1:3). The preamble was first introduced in the constitution in 1967, both to affirm that the names "The Protestant Episcopal Church in the United States of America" and "The Episcopal Church" designated the same church, and to place that church in the wider Anglican context. The change in the constitution made at that General Convention was introduced by the Mutual Responsibility Committee to the Committee on Structure in 1964. Thus, the definition was made by the committee whose primary concern was our inter-Anglican partnerships. Much of the language of this section of the preamble was drawn from resolution 49 of the Lambeth Conference of 1930.

7. Hodgson, *Revisioning the Church,* 21.

8. Ibid., 37.

9. Howe, *Anglicanism and The Universal Church,* 28.

10. "Primate" is the name given to the Archbishop, Presiding Bishop, President Bishop, Prime Bishop, etc. who in each autonomous regional church in the Anglican Communion is "prime" or "first" among the bishops of a province.

11. See McGeary, Martin, and Rosenthal, eds., *A Transforming Vision,* 157. Resolution 29 acknowledges the official end of the schism.

12. See Howe, *Anglicanism and the Universal Church,* 240–46, for a detailed account of the communion-wide debate; and McGeary, Martin, and Rosenthal, eds., *A Transforming Vision,* 32–33, for an overview of the last communion-wide discussion of continued issues regarding the ordination of women in some, but not all, provinces and dioceses.

13. A bit of Anglican nomenclature needs defining here: "Province" is used to name a regional autonomous church in the Anglican Communion (e.g., the Province of the Church of Kenya), while some provinces are themselves divided internally and call those internal divisions provinces (e.g., the Province of York and the Province of Canterbury in the Church of England and the nine domestic provinces in the Episcopal Church).

14. McGeary, Martin, and Rosenthal, eds., *A Transforming Vision,* iv (picture), 10.

15. The Faith and Order movement, out of which the World Council of Churches eventually would be formed, was energized by many Anglican participants, particularly Bishop Charles Henry Brent.

16. The Book of Common Prayer 1662 (Church of England), 613; The Book of Common Prayer 1979 (Episcopal Church), 868.

17. The Book of Common Prayer 1662 (Church of England), viii.

18. Ibid., 619.

19. Eliot, *Four Quartets*, 14.

20. In this regard, a careful reading of Paul's image of the church as the Body of Christ is in order (Rom. 12:4–8; 1 Cor. 12:3–31). My sense is that Paul is clear that a difference in function does not assume a difference in worth. He does suggest that some gifts are greater than others, but the greatest—love—is available to all.

21. Again, I refer the reader to Bosch, "The Emergence of a Postmodern Paradigm," *Transforming Mission*, 349–62.

22. See, for example, McFague, *The Body of God*.

23. Preface to the Book of Common Prayer 1549 and subsequent eds.

CHAPTER 3

THEOLOGY ROOTED IN THE INCARNATION

Theological reflection on the nature of God and on God's engagement with humankind in Jesus Christ has produced doctrines meant to inform and mold our faith. The methods used in this reflection can tell us a great deal about what sort of thing these doctrines are and how a particular faith community uses them. When a consistent method is used, such reflection tells us something about how a community views itself. Of course such an inquiry is bound to be incomplete, since theological reflection is forever in process. But inquiry into the theological method of Anglicanism should help us to get a bearing on why Anglicans seem to have a somewhat different sense of theological matters than, say, Lutherans or Roman Catholics. In turn, that method might tell us something about the extent to which Anglicans have a shared sense experience in the faith. The question is this: *Is there an Anglican Method, and does it contribute to Anglican self-understanding and sense of mission?*

THE INCARNATION IN ANGLICAN THEOLOGICAL METHOD

It sometimes happens that particular church groupings are seen to be fascinated with one or another doctrinal approach as a guiding principle. Such seems to be the case with Anglicanism. A wide range of theologians support the notion that Anglicans favor a theology that has as a *guiding principle* the experience, and often the doctrine, of the Incarnation.[1]

Dewi Morgan, in *Agenda for Anglicans*, begins his discussion of regional and national churches by quoting Dr. Eainar Molland, who said,

> If selection was to be made of a particular doctrine as especially characteristic of the Anglican Communion as a whole, it would certainly be the theology of the Incarnation. . . .If the Orthodox Church is "the Church of Easter," or the Lutheran "the Church of Good Friday," the Anglican Church may be described as "the Church of Christmas."[2]

Urban Holmes, in *What is Anglicanism?* also sees the Incarnation as the beginning point for Anglican theological sensibilities. He describes three characteristics of the Anglican understanding of the Incarnation:

(1) "The Incarnation means that God created everything that is. . . . The Incarnation is the ultimate act of creation."

(2) "The Incarnation means that sin cannot be explained by identifying it with matter or the physical world. . . .Sin is in the person or the community."

(3) "The Incarnation embraces the totality of life. It is the doctrine which undergirds the Anglican commitment to sensibility, the openness to the entire experience with all its conflict and ambiguity."[3]

Archbishop Michael Ramsey, in *The Anglican Spirit*, also spoke to the peculiar Anglican stress on the Incarnation:

> There is a divine reason present in the universe, operating in lots of different ways, whereby God bears witness to His own presence and activity. This indwelling of divine reason in the created world operates especially in the mind and the conscience of men and women. Thus revelation is a divine activity that evokes and calls for our own powers of reason and conscience, because those powers of reason and conscience are themselves God-given.
>
> That aspect of revelation is strongly present in Hooker's Laws . . . It was that line of thought, I think, that tended to

> push the Incarnation into first place in Anglican theology. It
> would be a bit of an oversimplification to say (but perhaps
> not too much of one) that in Anglican theology through the
> centuries the Incarnation has been a more central and
> prominent doctrine than that of the cross and redemption,
> and certainly more so than justification or predestination.[4]

Ramsey argued that, from the outset, the distinctively Anglican
line of theological inquiry was guided by an understanding of the Incarnation that gave a special place to the powers of reason and conscience.
Anglicans, who affirm the role of reason, can do so because the divine
logos, or reason, is what is incarnated in the created order and can be
known, since it "informs the conscience and reason of men and
women."[5]

Given the perceived sensibility of Anglicans as informed by the
Incarnation in a central way, we can understand why the question of
theological method is so important for us. The Incarnation, as a given
of faith, grounds our thinking about God in an empirical context. Thus
reasoning, as well as revelation, is a basis for theological work.

Anglicans have held that scripture, tradition, and reason all inform
our theological work, and our method consists in building from each of
these elements toward a unifying whole. Scripture has primacy in this
triad. Nothing can be held as essential to the faith that cannot be
proved or shown compatible with Holy Scripture. The same is not said
for tradition and reason. Yet these too can be applied to scripture, so
that scripture itself is understood with greater clarity.

All reformed faith places scripture in a special place. It is the final
arbiter of theological issues. Most reformed faith groups would consider the church to be an informing agent, either by way of the indwelling
of the Holy Spirit, or by way of the community of believers over time.
But there is great difficulty with the notion that reason can be a major
informing agent for faith. This is in part because *reason* is a slippery
word—it applies to a wide range of activities, some quite self-justify-
ing and self-glorifying, others quite narrowly focused. My sense is that
Anglicans would contend that sometimes reason resonates with the
work and effects of the Creator in such a way that reason alone brings
insight and information about God as our source and sustenance.

REASON IN ANGLICAN METHOD

Anglicans place the powers of reason in the wider context of faithfulness to the divine *logos* out of which it arose. The *logos* manifests itself in the Incarnation. Thus, the understanding of the Incarnation becomes particularly important as a beginning place for theological method. It grounds reason in a way that binds the particular to the universal, the material to the spiritual, the body to spirit in a unifying way. Of course this understanding of the Incarnation is quite ancient in the church. When Irenaeus argued in the second century against the Gnostic heresies, which were heresies of rational dualism, his defense drew heavily on his understanding of the Incarnation, which proposed that all experience reflects God's manifestation of self. His thinking became formative in the development of the doctrine of the Incarnation.

The issue of method is closely linked to the issue of authority. On what information are we to apply our rational powers, and what is the arbitrator for those powers? If, because we all participate in the *logos,* we can think from within God's manifestation of self, what guides us? What has God given us that provides an authoritative basis for our faith? The Anglican formulation of an answer to the question of authority in method came to be cast in terms of the famous appeal to scripture, reason, and tradition (also called antiquity). Here reason, as an information base, is not a method, but a product. Reason informs our belief because its conclusions, if true, constitute a body of knowledge derived from the same source, the *logos* of God that is found in the Incarnation of Jesus as the Christ. The information grows from a framework in which the Incarnation, as the union of the material and spiritual, is the focal point. Information can be and is derived from nature as well as from abstract thought, history as well as ritual story-telling, culture as well as canon. This means that reason makes of all natural science and natural history a canon which can inform our faith. Anglicans hold these three avenues of authoritative information continually in tension, never completely giving in to the humanism and rationalism on the one hand or the *sola scriptura* position of the more radical reformers, on the other.

The charge arose after the First World War, and again after the Second, that liberalism and rationalism had failed the human community.

The charge that reason is dangerously limited, both as a power and as an information base, needs to be addressed. How is it that Anglicans can hold up the Incarnation as a basis on which to model the bridging of the gulf between our finitude and God's infinitude, between our injustice and God's justice? Surely it was not the Incarnation that provided an adequate context for faith. It was not God's *presence* in Jesus Christ, but God's *action* in Christ that was primary to our salvation. It was not Incarnation, but Atonement, theology that needed to be accented.

Charles Gore, writing in the early part of this century, suggested an answer. He developed the idea of *kenosis*, the self-limitation of the divine wisdom of God in the Incarnation in Jesus. Michael Ramsey describes the notion in this way:

> While Jesus was an infallible revelation of God, he had a mind that was subject to the genuine conditions of his time. . . .Anglican teachers of that period (Gore, et.al.) did not hesitate to combine a belief in the divine Christ with a belief in Christ's total participation in the conditions of human life.[6]

If that self-limitation was present in the Incarnation, and the Incarnation is the model for our engagement with the powers of God present in our reason and conscience, then we should expect such limitations to exist for all human struggles to do or know God's will.

There are always hesitations by Anglicans to make of reason more than it can bear. Ramsey picks up on the suggestion from the writers of *Lux Mundi* that true doctrine—right thinking—is for Anglicans a matter of progressive disclosure and understanding. "Under the guidance of the Holy Spirit, we are given fresh understandings and fresh articulation of what has been revealed originally in all kinds of hidden seeds."[7]

Incarnational thinking does not presume that we can be triumphalist about reason, but only that reason can be an avenue for revealing what was hidden. For faithful people, reason is never an independent operation, uninformed by scripture or tradition. The guidance of the Holy Spirit is meant to complete and complement reason, bound as it is by the specifics of Incarnation, in specific persons and in specific times. Reason is forever limited, even as Jesus was limited by being incarnate as a specific person in time.

The danger persists that Anglicans can adopt an easy incarnational approach to avoid the terror of confronting the reality of sin and limit, too easily assuming the attitude of progressive liberalism. Urban Holmes speaks to the danger of easy incarnationalism and suggests the corrective of a more radical incarnationalism:

> The danger in Anglicanism's emphasis upon the incarnation is what happens when we hold to the doctrine, but sanitize its implications. [We get] a debased Anglicanism, which confuses cultural ideals and values with the mind of God. The doctrine of the Incarnation supports the conviction that Christ transforms culture, rather than a projection of the culture. Whenever we allow ourselves a certain smudginess and complacency [our religion] becomes very mushy and we encourage clergy who are dilettantes and laity who are bigots. It is a disease, which has cursed us from the beginning in England and knows every corner of the church.

If we are true to radical incarnationalism, then our religion keeps us on edge. We cannot escape the terror of the darkness within and we know that the only remedy to evil is the cross of the Christ. The Incarnation, God's becoming a servant to be one of us, is a sacrifice, of which Christ's Passion is the moment of fulfillment.[8]

REASON AND THE NOTION OF PROGRESS

Anglican theology has held reason to be an informing source for faith. It has done so in the face of considerable criticism from both reformed and catholic parties. But perhaps the most damning criticism has arisen from those who believe that the term reason is too easily identified with liberal or "politically correct" thinking. The appeal to reason was seen too often to be an appeal to what reasonable people would do (i.e., people of our sort). It has been suggested, for example, that British empiricism in its more positivist trappings was singularly silent and unhelpful in its ability to provide any commentary on or analysis of either the rise of Nazism or the end of colonialism in the period between the two World Wars.

Getting out of the trap of reason, that it has no challenge to itself as self-glorifying, is a problem for the Anglican method, in which scripture, tradition, and reason all play a part. Reason is always incomplete, but does not know itself to be so. Yet reason is a bridge between what we can read in the created order and what we can know of the Creator. It is part of Anglican theological method because it provides an incarnational bridge. Reason concerns only what we know. Although "when the perfect comes, the imperfect will pass away" (1 Cor. 13:10), for the time being, reason and the knowledge that derives from it are part of who we are. Reason is filled with the provisionality that pervades all of life. The treasures are indeed in earthen vessels.

ANGLICAN METHOD AS COMPREHENSIVE AND PRAGMATIC

Anglican theological method concerns itself with the possibility of a comprehensive faith, one in which the unbridgeable distance between God and the creation is bridged. Theological engagement must always address the problem that the encounter with God is beyond reason alone, and that therefore there is either too little time or too great a mental distance for comprehension to be complete. The Anglican response to that fact has very often been to try to find a way to continue working at comprehension anyway, by trying to find a method to ground belief when knowledge is incomplete. So for Anglicans, the question becomes one of trying to find a method for arriving at a continuing approximation of the truth, a process for attempting comprehension.

The charge has been laid that Anglicans have avoided the central and beginning point of faith, which is that we stand convicted and in need of salvation. Rather than acknowledging the depravity of humankind and responding to that, it would appear that Anglicans leap too quickly to the hope of union with God. That would be true if there were not clearly fixed in our faithfulness the image of the cross as intimately one with the Incarnation itself. The stress on the Incarnation is not an avoidance of the cross, but rather an effort to know the One who died for us. We ourselves become followers and betrayers, mourners and those filled with joy.

The Incarnation, as an experiential matrix both in its historical concreteness and now as a spiritual event, becomes the basis for theological engagement. It does indeed assure that the gulf is bridgeable. We can know God in Jesus Christ; we can know that the truth shall set us free (cf. John 8:32b),[9] even if it is always known provisionally.

It is experience with the Christ that is the core to this assurance, but such experience is not easily reduced to doctrine. Rather, it is always filled with what T.S. Eliot called "sensibility." Urban Holmes calls this "taking into account the whole of an experience—ambiguity and all. . . .We [Anglicans] are at our best when we acknowledge the penultimate nature of our answers to the character of God and his will for us."[10]

It is the sense that all theological conclusions are *provisional* that seems to pervade Anglican inquiry. According to Ramsey, it is present in Hooker's belief

> in authority mingled with a great distrust of infallibility. He is ready to believe, certainly, in what God has shown and done, but equally ready to shrink from claims for the infallibility of the language in which God's revelation is at any time expressed. A sentence of Hooker expressed this: "two things there are that trouble these latter times: one is that the Church of Rome can not, another is that Geneva will not, err."[11]

Method becomes, for Anglicans, the way by which the matrix of experience is continually revisited as a means of gathering a wider sense of our unity with God. We begin our theological work with the belief that we have a base of information, a contextual environment in which to work with this information and an understanding that conclusions from this work are always provisional.

Anglican theological method is shot through and through with discourse in community, with mutuality. It assumes that, out of the encounters with the scriptures of the Christian community, its traditions, and the give and take of rational discourse, there must come a movement toward the apprehension of the truth.

The truth is also experienced in an immediate way in the awareness of the Incarnation, our spiritual knowledge of God in Christ, our knowledge of God in all of creation, our awareness of God in us. Anglican method assumes that the encounter with the world and other persons is one of mutual engagement. It is also known, negatively, in the deep awareness of the suffering caused by our limitations and our greed, and in our unwillingness to encounter the world and others in mutuality. The experience of discourse and mutuality has become itself a basis for confidence in the possibilities of a method of comprehensiveness.

The Anglican desire to be comprehensive is based on the knowledge of our limitations, on the experience of deeply sinful engagement in religious disputes, and on a desire to engage a community larger than the limits of our own doctrinal prejudices. The Anglican willingness to include within its community persons of widely different theological opinions has often been criticized. The bishops at Lambeth in 1948 had this to say in response to that criticism:

> Comprehensiveness is an attitude of mind which Anglicans have learned from the thought-provoking controversies of their history. . . . Comprehensiveness demands agreement on fundamentals, while tolerating disagreement on matters in which Christians may differ without feeling the necessity of breaking communion. In the mind of an Anglican, comprehensiveness is not a compromise. Nor is it to bargain one truth for another. It is not a sophisticated word for syncretism. Rather it implies that the apprehension of truth is a growing thing: we only gradually succeed in "knowing the truth" . . . for we believe that in leading us into the truth the Holy Spirit may have some surprises in store for us in the future as he has had in the past.[12]

The question "Is there an Anglican method?" can be answered positively. Anglican theological method at least involves the following:

(1) It is grounded in the Incarnation;

(2) it is built on information derived from scripture, tradition, and reason;

(3) it understands this information in the context of experience; and

(4) it assumes engagement in a process of apprehension that assumes community and comprehensiveness.

Anglicans have often noted that prayer shapes belief: we begin first with prayer, and follow with belief. What common prayer brings to theology is the ability to acquire habits of experience. Inquiry, for Anglicans, takes place not in a vacuum, but in the struggle to attain a state of belief sufficient to our common experience in prayer. Thus, as Anglicans, we have not so much produced new theologies as struggled to be faithful to existing theologies as they are lived out in prayer and community.

It is my sense that Anglicans do have a theological method, one that does not tend to produce surprising new religious principles, but one that builds on the experience of people of faith. The Incarnation stands at the focal point of this method, for the implication of the Incarnation is that the knowledge of God can be known by experiencing this one human being, Jesus the Messiah. The pragmatic process—drawing together information, experience, and a spiritual sensibility that knows that the whole is greater than the provisional knowledge of the moment—provides a method that serves Anglicans, and indeed the whole of Christianity, well.

I began this exploration by saying that *Anglicans define themselves by their experience.* Our experience has been of fellowship, of something like a religious order in the church universal or catholic. In it our primary ground is the Incarnation, our primary informing sources as broadly comprehensive as possible, our faith contextual, and the marks of our life based in the ongoing witness of the whole faithful community and our fellowship itself.

We are a provisional people, as Anglicans, within the certainty of the Kingdom of God, willing at our best to look always beyond our own limitations. We accept as part of our experience that our life as a community is responsible to, and finds justification in, the future of God's mission. The challenge now is to ask ourselves just what of our experience will contribute to that mission.

Is it possible, given our experience, to envision a future vocation for Anglicans? I believe it *is* possible and, given the circumstances, necessary to do so. Since the time of Constantine, and until recently, the fragmentation of Christianity has had its sources in disagreements *within* the Christian culture. The fragmentation of the church, now occurring in a western culture that is post-Christian, and in other cultures in which Christianity has been a minority religion or an agency of the imperial west, is a fragmentation to which the cultures themselves contribute. There is no unifying culture and no unifying theology. The hope for a solid reference point in either culture or theology has been crushed under the weight of internal dissent in the church and pluralism in the cultures in which it moves. The proclamation of the gospel is often now in the hands of organizations and individuals for whom the experience of working within the parameters of a Christian society is unknown.

The results, of course, are mixed. At best, new orders, sects, and churches will arise to witness and proclaim Jesus as the Christ in ways we might never imagine. These may be both creative and corrective. At worst, orders, sects, and churches will use Christian language to further ends unrelated to the faith received or known by those of us who now call ourselves Christian. More and more people, of course, will simply give up on the confusing range of claims made by rival Christian groups. The needs for spiritual sustenance will be met elsewhere, and hopes for a better life in the present will be met by secular means.[13] It will be the particular witness of historic Christian communities, like the Anglican churches, to maintain the continuity of faith in ways that inform the present and contribute to future unity in Christ.

Countering this fragmentation is a primary task of apostolic ministry, that is, of ministry that returns repeatedly to the earliest testimony to Jesus and to the struggles of women and men through the ages to understand and apply themselves to that testimony. Anglican thinkers have always appealed to scripture and the earliest of the teachings of the church available for primary insight. They do so believing that reflection on these, in the light of reason and in the context of our being a peculiar people, bounded by the particulars of culture and history, will give us a comprehensive sense of what God would have us do. In so doing, we have appealed to the one other historical period in which Christianity did not provide the culture in which it was proclaimed. During all the upheavals of the period from the beginnings of the Christian community until the end of the persecutions in the early fourth century, the central question seemed as clear as it does today.

In the pre-Constantinian empire, the question for Christians was Jesus' own, "Who do you say that I am?" And now, in a post-Christian society, the question is the same again. And it must be answered, as it was then, by individuals without state or cultural sanctions. Our fellowship in Christian community will be the only place to gather courage to answer the question we will finally answer alone. We are at the edge of a new age of martyrdom, in which the faith will be tested not so much by the monolithic state as by the polylithic, pluralistic culture. Christian witness will be met not by the crushing weight of the state, but by the stones thrown by pious followers of what will ironically seem to be Christian purity codes.

We Anglicans have tried to answer Jesus' question "Who do you say that I am?" in our own seemingly untidy way by returning repeatedly to a "religion of the Incarnation"[14] and to Peter's answer, "You are the Messiah, the Son of the living God" (Matt. 16:15–16). Anglicans have mostly assumed the traditional understanding that the phrase "the Son of the living God" implicates us in a religion in which the belief in the Incarnation is central and is expressed in terms of the hopes of people in community. The "Son of God," who can be attested to by the individual Peter, is therefore also the hope of the people Israel.

Anglicans, too, have for the most part been moved by the "why" of the Incarnation, not the "how"—that is, by the Incarnation itself, not the doctrine. In working out a sense of the "why" of the Incarnation, Anglicans have understood the Incarnation as a comprehensive activity. Belief in the specific engagement of God with the created order in the person of Jesus is a sign of much wider understandings of the relation of God and creation, that relation being one of *compassionate love.*

I believe a strong case can be made that Anglicans continue the witness: (1) to the centrality of the Incarnation; (2) to its implications for the whole people; and (3) to its comprehensive affirmation of God's engagement in creation, which engagement I believe we can legitimately call compassionate.

Our vocation is to make this threefold witness. That is, I believe we are called to an envisioning theology of incarnation, to a community of mutuality, and to a life of compassionate engagement. Nothing about this vision or vocation is in any way our own. Indeed I believe part of the implication of this witness is that Anglican Churches will serve a provisional function on the way to a unity they cannot contain. Yet what we have to do will be an important contribution to the life in faithful obedience to Jesus, who said, "I came that they may have life, and have it abundantly" (John 10:10). His being among us, our life together, and God's abundant compassion are the bedrock of our witness—and not of ours only, but of the whole faithful people of God.

The reader is aware, I am sure, of the considerable space given to thinking about the Incarnation, both as the historically important beginning point for Anglican theology, and as the practical immediate departure point for much of what constitutes our best hope for the future. I believe it is a topic of considerable importance to Anglican thought, and here we can really do nothing more than sketch out the broad outlines of its effect on the way Anglicans do their theological and ecclesial work.

A PRELIMINARY NOTE ON THE WORD *INCARNATION*

Most of what follows in this section is directly dependent on two extraordinary books: John Hick's *The Myth of God Incarnate* and Francis Young's *The Making of the Creeds.* They are immensely helpful in charting the progress in the development of the idea of the Incarnation. Quite independently of their challenging conclusions, they suggest that from the outset it is helpful to make a distinction between various strata of the word *Incarnation.* The word refers to:

(1) an aspect of the experience of those who knew Jesus;

(2) a belief that grew in the community of the early church about Jesus;

(3) a description of his work both in his life and death and as the Risen Lord; and

(4) a doctrine of the church.

Part of the confusion that accompanies any discussion of the Incarnation arises because these strata are confused.

Testimony and reference for these strata can be gathered on each level:

(1) The followers of Jesus in his lifetime are remembered to have made at least some experientially based statements supporting his being not just an anointed one, but also the Son of God. There is the beginning. Not all these statements assume uniqueness or necessarily imply Incarnation, but some point in that direction. They range from Peter's statement, "You are the Christ, the Son of the living God" (Matt. 16:16) to the centurion at the cross, "Surely this was the Son of God"

(2) The beginning of the Gospel of John clearly references the belief in an "enfleshment" (John 1:14), one that is open to wider incarnational implications.

(3) The assertion is made of Jesus' work in 2 Corinthians, that in Jesus the Christ (the name bridging the earthly and resurrected activity of the Lord), God was in the world reconciling the world to himself (2 Cor. 5:19).

(4) The beginnings of credal formulations, culminating in the Nicene Creed, describe Jesus as "being of one substance with the Father" and as one "who was enfleshed. . .and became a human being," that is, incarnated.

The belief that Jesus Christ is the Word or Wisdom of God, or God made Incarnate, lies somewhere *between* the experience of Jesus and the creeds and undergirds the doctrine of the Incarnation. It is a belief that is particular, a claim about a unique person. While it may have universal application, becoming a claim about all people, or all people of a given group, it begins by being about a particular person, in a particular location. That is, the belief in the Incarnation grows from the specifics of the experience of the immediate followers, from reflective and faithful reasoning at a later point, and from reflection on the life, death, and resurrection of Jesus Christ seen as a whole. But the belief is *prior* to the doctrine.

The belief in the Incarnation is about the particularity of the presence of God in Jesus, as a whole event. It is about the *work* of Jesus. Birth and death specify the range of one part of that total work. Incarnational theology is sometimes understood as being about the birth of Jesus Christ, and Atonement theology as being about the specific concern to give meaning to the death of Jesus Christ on the cross. Yet when we speak of our belief that Jesus Christ is God Incarnate we are talking neither of his birth nor of his death, but rather about God being present in the *whole of the work* of Jesus Christ.

THE INCARNATION AND THE ATONEMENT

I have suggested in several places that the Incarnation is the beginning point for much of Anglican thought, but it is not the beginning place for all Christians. Indeed it would appear that it is the cross and Resurrection that make up the central event around which many Christians form theology and faithfulness. On some level, of course, Anglicans do, too. After all, Easter, as the celebration of the Resurrection in which the death on the cross is overcome, is the great Christian feast. According to our Prayer Book understanding, all Sundays are reflections of that Easter event.[15]

The Resurrection of Jesus Christ is often seen as a paradigm for our own eternity, for our overcoming sin and the grave. It is a sign of things to come, and a sign of the way out of sin and death. It is a compelling image, all the more so because it seems also to point to our resolution now to live an amended life. And so, living in the light of the Resurrection has come to mean living with the desire to show the fruits of an amended life, that is, to be morally upright. Resurrection faith, with its self-examination, confession, being made new, prayer and fasting and feasting, sharing in Holy Eucharist, has been a gift of immense value to Christian life and spirituality. And yet there are several problems with the great stress on Resurrection as the central and exclusive core of faithfulness:

(1) The emphasis on the cross and Resurrection, and on our death to sin and redemption in new life, has led to complex doctrines of the Atonement.[16] Faith in the cross as the instrument of atonement and the Resurrection as its confirmation, is often bolstered by claiming Jesus as the unique and only incarnation of God on the basis of those atonement doctrines themselves. Although Peter's witness at Pentecost (Acts 2:22–24) was to the whole of Jesus' work, four hundred years later the Nicene Creed would not mention a single thing about Jesus' healing, preaching, or engagement with the world. Later atonement theology makes little of who Jesus was in his life and rather it concentrates on what God did in Jesus on the cross.

Yet many other Christians more strongly emphasize the life of Jesus, and his death as part of that life rather than as a result of a cosmic drama. Belief in Jesus as the Incarnation of the Word or Wisdom of God is the result of what we understand he was about, in the particulars of his life, as the compassion of God made real in the world.[17] The uniqueness of Jesus as God's only Son is not a logical requirement of such a doctrine, as if God's compassion could only be made real through the particular person of Jesus. Rather, the uniqueness is in the matching of Jesus' compassion and our allegiance to him in that compassion. When Jesus says, "As the Father has sent me, so I send you"

(John 20:21), we are called to follow him in the way of compassionate action. Indeed, the reference to Jesus being the "first fruits" (1 Cor. 15.23) is an indication that God's indwelling compassion is incarnated in other persons who follow him.[18]

There is then a dissonance between these two, between *cross and Resurrection* with its sin and redemption cycle and accompanying religion of Atonement, and *Incarnation and cross* and its works and witness of compassion, with its accompanying religion of the Incarnation. The theology of the cross and Resurrection has come to imply concerns for eternity and judgment, and this theology seems to call for a morally careful response. The Resurrection is usually seen to confirm that Jesus is God uniquely present, and it is therefore identified completely with God's action and final judgment.

Incarnational living carries the possibility of our sharing in our Lord's daring engagement in compassion. It assumes that the signs of God's presence are seen in the "fruits" of behavior, in active particularity. Jesus said that his followers might do even greater things than he (John 14:21), suggesting that God's presence would be known in them as well. One might argue that it is precisely that incarnational response of active particularity that got Jesus executed and issued in the Resurrection as the final "sign of Jonah."

Yet in the minds of many Christians, the Resurrection has become a reason not for the confirmation of God's sanction of incarnational risk taking, but a sign for careful judgment. This pattern or paradigm of the Resurrection seems most often to have been stressed as a guarantor of our eternal life, particularly following death, and a warning that things done for good or ill now have eternal consequences. It has become an argument for purity codes.[19]

I believe the Resurrection needs to be placed in a different context, where compassion has better soil in which to grow. That soil is the Incarnation. Seen by eyes that have beheld the presence of God incarnate in the world, the Resurrection is a confirmation of God's lovingkindness. Even death could not take him away from us.

(2) The Gospels are mostly about the work and ministry of Jesus as the Messiah, up to and including the cross. The Resurrection is a sign. It does not stand alone as the center. If there is a center, it is most

arguably the crucifixion as the crisis following on a life of compassion-ate engagement with humanity, not the Resurrection.[20] Even then, John Dominic Crossan has argued that in the first two centuries it was the compassion itself that was most remembered, particularly the compassion of the open meal and healing, and not the cross at all.[21] Indeed, if the Gospels were dramas (which I concede they are not) the Resurrection would be the resolution of the play, not the crisis or turning point. The stress on Resurrection has led to a confusion of signs and the thing signified. The thing *signified* is the whole work of Jesus the Christ, of the Word or Wisdom of God with us.

(3) The Resurrection is a faith event described in a particular cultural context. It was understood to underscore and signal the reality of God's reign. But in its interpretation to the wider Greek and Roman world, it became a signal for our eternity, and for the reign of a new moral order replacing older ones. God's reign became a moral reality, because when one was made fully aware of the Almighty's power and one's own sin, there could only be total reliance on God's grace and mercy. God's rule is acknowledged in the realm of judgment. Because the Resurrection shows that death is not the end, judgment will surely come. In a strange way, the Resurrection became a reason for damning all those who do not believe—rather than a reason for believing that Jesus is the Incarnation of the Word or Wisdom of God, and that we, too, might be children of God.

The church has proposed moral implications of the Resurrection that have little warrant in Scripture. God's mercy and justice can be felt and known without it. The easy yoke and light burden Jesus claimed was ours has become heavy, sometimes tragic, sometimes strangely silly. What began as the wonder of God's presence among us became the terror of God's judgment on us. That God's incarnation and compassion working in the world should be central—and our actions encouraged as possible reflections of God's reign—is rarely emphasized. And that lack of attention is tragic.

The Anglican concern to keep the Incarnation as a central focus is of great value to those who see the continuing need for balance in the understanding of the good news. Anglicans are not alone in this attempt, of course, but we are amazingly consistent in the desire to lift up the experience of the Incarnation.

ANGLICAN SOURCES FOR INCARNATIONAL THEOLOGY

Given the overwhelming fascination with the moral implications of the Atonement—particularly in the formative period of the English Reformation, when thinking was dominated by European motifs and concerns—the continuing Anglican theological work on the Incarnation is quite astounding. Very early theologians, Irenaeus and Athanasius among them, did much of the groundwork for this thinking. These theologians did the work that preceded the development of the *doctrine* of the Incarnation. They dealt with the idea itself, by which I mean the notion based on some sort of experience, that Jesus is God, or God's Word in human form, and conversely humanity in God's form. Irenaeus, early on in the development of doctrine (ca. 180 AD), and Athanasius almost 140 years later (ca. 318 AD), when the doctrinal controversies had reached great heights, both wrote from the context of *wonder* at the experience of the Incarnation.

IRENAEUS AND THE IDEA OF RECAPITULATION

In *The Scandal of the Incarnation,* under the heading, "Incarnation as Recapitulation," Hans Urs von Balthasar has collected some of Irenaeus's writing on the Incarnation as *experienced.* The experience of Jesus as the Incarnation of God "made the whole creation new." That experience was described as the creation being set aright, having the same mind as its Creator. To express this setting-aright, the expression "recapitulation" was used. The English word *recapitulation* represents the Greek *anakephalaiosis,* used by the author of Ephesians to express God's plan in Jesus, "to bring everything together under Christ as head, everything in the heavens and everything on earth" (Eph. 1:10). Von Balthasar understands Irenaeus's use of this word to mean not only that Christ is head of the world, but also that "in Him everything becomes clear and has meaning," including "the reconciliation of the world and God, of nature and grace, which has its foundation in the one Incarnation."[22]

Several most remarkable statements are gathered in this context: "He became the Son of Man to accustom man to receive God and God to dwell in man. In His immeasurable love, He became what we are, in order to make us what He is."[23]

The Incarnation is both a way of getting us accustomed to the idea that God can be received—that God can dwell in us—and the idea that the Incarnation is an act of "immeasurable love," or compassion, so that we can become "what He is." It is perhaps unclear as doctrine, but it is wonderfully clear as a profound religious experience. Here Irenaeus is not arguing for a doctrine of the Incarnation, but rather for an experienced reality. The Incarnation is the way beyond the gulf that separates God from nature.

The experience of the Incarnation for most of us is precisely the insight that "God was in Christ, reconciling the world unto himself" (2 Cor 5:19, KJV). This insight is gained experientially by our personal "turning around," in which we see the "recapitulation" in ourselves and Christ as our head.

ATHANASIUS ON THE INCARNATION OF THE WORD OF GOD

One hundred forty years after Irenaeus, Athanasius wrote of the Incarnation as well. His work also arose from experience, not from abstracted theological investigation. The experience was that of martyrdom, suffered by friends and family in the last years of the Roman Empire before Constantine. Athanasius noted that if we were not blinded by our own limitations, we should see God's image in ourselves, and therefore the Word, and creation itself would be a sufficient incarnation of God for our knowledge of the Word. He said,

> God knew the limitation of mankind, you see; and though the grace of being made in His Image was sufficient to give them knowledge of the Word and through Him of the Father, as a safeguard against their neglect of this grace, He provided the works of creation also as a means by which the Maker might be known.[24]

For Athanasius, the Incarnation in Jesus Christ becomes a necessity, as it did for Irenaeus, because we are not able to grasp the Incarnation of God in ourselves or in all of creation. The argument for God's Incarnation in Jesus Christ is that it is the only way to bring the matter home—that there *is* a participation between God and nature, such that reality (nature) is shot through and through with God's Word.

In *De incarnatione verbi Dei,* Athanasius argues that the Incarnation is the central focus for Christian belief. The doctrines of the Resurrection, the Atonement, and the cross are all secondary to his central point. The Incarnation of the Word of God in Jesus Christ is an act of a loving God who wishes that we see the Word in all the created order. Knowing that we do not see, God confronts us with the Word made flesh in a particular part of the creation, in human form, in the person of Jesus Christ. What drives the Incarnation-based believer is not primarily the need for propitiation for our sins, but confrontation with the fact of God's presence in all of reality. Athanasius asks, "If the Word of God is in the universe, which is a body, and has entered into it in its every part, what is there surprising or unfitting in our saying that He has entered also into human nature?"[25]

> The Word of God thus acted consistently in assuming a body and using a human instrument to vitalize the body. He was consistent in working through man to reveal Himself everywhere, as well as through the other parts of His creation, so that nothing was left void of His Divinity and knowledge. For I take up now the point I made before, namely that the Savior did this in order that He might fill all things everywhere with the knowledge of Himself, just as they are already filled with His presence, even as the Divine Scripture says, "the whole universe was filled with the knowledge of the Lord."[26]

Here again is the sense, seen earlier in Irenaeus, that it is the incarnate Christ that sets things aright, so that all creation, humanity included, is recapitulated in the Word.

Setting things aright may be a form of atonement, but the picture is quite different from the grim doctrine one usually associates with Atonement theology. Atonement doctrine seems to have developed in two directions. Either it posits the problem of sin as condemnation, for which the solution is substitutional restitution in Jesus Christ, or it posits the problem of sin as misguided sight, for which the solution is to regain one's sight by acquiring the mind of Christ (recapitulation). The first of these alternatives is what we normally think of when we speak of Atonement theology. This second is a process of *participation* in God, becoming partners in the Incarnation. It is atonement by recapitulation.

In this connection A. M. Allchin's short study, *Participation in God,* is most helpful. He begins by quoting Athanasius, "God became man so that man might become God."[27] His interest is in the possibility that "man might become God." This he calls the doctrine of deification. Allchin sees this exploration as a way beyond the impasse of current western thought that has "given up all thought of the search for God." Those seeking

> a saving knowledge of the ultimate truth of things . . . have abandoned the Christian tradition that seems only to talk about God without showing any way to realize his presence. Christianity, which contains at its heart a message about the reconciliation and union of humanity with God, seems to them no longer to convey the mystery of which it speaks.[28]

It is that reconciliation and union that the Book of Common Prayer concerns itself with when it speaks of the mission of the church. "What is the mission of the Church?" the Catechism asks. "The mission of the Church is to restore all people to unity with God and each other in Christ."[29] This restorative work is deification by way of reconciliation and union. The particular character of the Incarnation in Jesus Christ, then, is that it presents the image for us, so that we may become like him; it sets the stage for our deification.

The way in which Allchin speaks of this is in terms of the idea of *participation in God.* His source for this notion is found in the ancient church teachers, and in the work of Richard Hooker. Hooker saw the Incarnation as both the core of sacramental theology and participation in God.[30] In *The Laws of Ecclesiastical Polity,* Hooker said, "No good is infinite, but only God; therefore he is our felicity and bliss. Moreover desire leadeth unto union with what it desireth. If then in him we are blessed, it is by force of participation and conjunction with him."[31]

Allchin believes we should re-evaluate the traditions that led to the doctrines of the Trinity and the Incarnation. Much of modern criticism of these doctrines has proceeded, he says,

> from the supposition that the development of the doctrines of the Trinity and the Incarnation in the early Christian centuries marked the intrusion of abstract and alien Greek ways of thought into the power and simplicity of the original gospel message. It has been [Allchin's] purpose. . .to suggest

that the contrary is the case, that when these doctrines are seen in their true significance, in relation to the doctrine of man's deification in Christ through the Spirit, then they may be seen to express and safeguard the very heart of the New Testament message of the reconciliation and union of God and man.[32]

The idea of recapitulation as the human engagement with God helps explain why it is that Anglicans have been attracted to the Incarnation, both as a doctrine and as an experience. Emphasizing the doctrine of the Incarnation "tones down" the doctrine of the Atonement, making it less a vehicle for judgment and more a reach for union. At the same time, the Incarnation experience fosters a spirituality in which we are drawn toward God, not abased before God. Allchin sums up the experience of union and attraction this way:

At the heart of our world, at the heart of each one of us, God wills to dwell. . . .In the descent of God's joy into the center of our world, man's spirit leaps up into union with God's Spirit, the world's own power of life is released, its responsive and creative power rises up and participates in the eternal movement of love which is at the very heart of God himself.[33]

The Incarnation lives on in the experience, if only dimly known, of that union of God and humankind by which we may glimpse the full joy of eternity in the present.

CRANMER AND HOOKER ON THE INCARNATION

The central doctrine for the Reformation was that of justification by faith alone. It not only put an end to the economy of indulgences, but eliminated all social, political, and spiritual interchange from the economy of salvation. The implications of this doctrine were astounding, and they remain with us. A prayer in the Second Prayer Book of Edward VI, still part of the Rite I Eucharist in the American Prayer Book, is absolutely clear on the point that even reception of communion is not a work of merit or a means of justification: "Although we bee unworthy throughe oure manifolde sinnes to offre unto thee any Sacrifice, yet we beseche thee. . . ."[34] Works are dead. At the same time, the bidding prayer in the same service makes it clear that the church encourages reception of the sacrament: "I bydde you all that be here present, and beseche you for the Lord Jesus Christes sake, that ye will not refuse to come thereto, being so lovingly called and bidden of god hymselfe."[35]

If we are saved only by God's grace and mercy, and if no amount of good works can justify us before God, then why the bidding to the sacrament? In the former economy it might have made sense to have masses said for the dead, or to go regularly to church oneself. But why the sacrament, if we are justified only by faith? Of course we do these things because we are told to do so by Jesus. Yet if it is simply a matter of obedience, and obedience, like any other work, is no long part of the economy, would it finally make any difference to our salvation or our justification?

The answer Cranmer and Hooker provided to this quandary remains central to Anglican practice. The economy of salvation is in one sense a closed one: God gives, we embrace, God accepts. Work is not a factor in the equation. Yet work can be a faithful response of gratitude. Our work resonates with the dynamics of salvation and faith. It has a *sympathetic resonance.* My sense is that this hint, that our work is somehow in resonance with the great work of God in Christ, is central to the Anglican understanding of the sacraments. Works that are done without thought for reward, and done from the heart, become the expression of Christ in us.

Something like this is also central to Richard Hooker's understanding of the sacraments. Hooker, too, has to answer the question of just how sacraments are integrated into a theological scheme in which salvation rests with God's grace and mercy and our justification rests in faith. Hooker says, "Sacramentes are the powerfull instrumentes of God to eternall life. For as our naturall life consisteth in the union of the bodie with the soule; so our life supernaturall in the union of the soule with God."[36] The soul is the connector, the "mean betweene both which is both."[37] "The mean between both which is both" is first of all Christ, for Christ is "the union of the soule with God" in the profoundest way possible.

The understanding of the Incarnation becomes central to the understanding of the sacraments, for the Incarnation is the occasion for the complete resonance between God and humanity, the one place where the internal economy of salvation and the response of the heart exactly coincide. When Jesus, as human, responds to the grace of God by faith, it is with a completely open heart, with work that "does not count the cost." He is the full linking of the human and divine. This is what I understand Hooker to imply by talking about participation.

Hooker, like Cranmer, understood that the closed economy of salvation had to have a place of resonance if work of any sort was to have meaning, and that place of resonance is the soul. The resonance is a participation in the divine Trinity. Hooker says,

> For this cause the Apostle wisheth to the Church of Corinth the grace of our Lord Jesus Christ, and the love of God, and the felloweship of the holie Ghost. Which three St Peter comprehendeth in one, the *participation of divine nature.* Wee are therefore in God through Christ eternallie. . . ."[38]

This participation is by way of Jesus, who shares with us soul—*anima*—and who is moved to compassion as we are (as a gut response), and not as God is moved (a matter of mercy), but completely.

Hooker completes what Cranmer begins, providing a way to understand the sacraments in relation to the doctrine of justification by faith. A parallel can be drawn: *God's grace and our faith* stand to *works* as *Christ's effectual sacrifice once and for all* stands to *the sacraments as enacted.* In neither case is our action causal. God's grace and our faith are what matter. What we do in action (works) cannot change that. The sacrifice of Christ is the atoning sacrifice; what we do cannot change that in the slightest.

Just as Cranmer suggested that our work is the result of a "true and lively faith," a matter of the heart, so Hooker suggests that our receiving the sacrament is a matter of an engagement of the heart with Christ in his atoning sacrifice. Hooker says, "For the sacramentes the verie same is true which Salomons wisdom observeth in the brasen serpent, "He that tourned towards it was not healed by the thinge he sawe, but by thee O savoir of all.'"[39] It is the participation with Christ in the sacrament that represents the grace *already and quite independently there* as part of the economy of salvation. While Hooker speaks of receiving the sacraments primarily as a matter of obedience, that obedience is itself a participation in the Divine. It is the response of the human heart to the heart of God.

Anglican theology was able to make the leap from the doctrine of justification by faith alone to a new context for the sacramental action. This was done by changing the object of sacramental action from good works to another purpose. The purpose of sacramental action became the desire to seek resonance to God's grace given once and for all. The sacraments become a matter of our joyful obedience, rather than our fruitless efforts to lift ourselves by our own bootstraps.

Anglicans have been quite willing to admit that the experience of the Incarnation, or of its effects, is not easily translated into theology. There are, of course, many paths that could be taken in trying to reason about the Incarnation. All begin with the work done by early theologians, and all reference the Reformation thinkers, particularly Richard Hooker. But in the twentieth century the basic division in the discussion of the Incarnation is between those who are concerned about the *efficacy of the doctrine* and those who are concerned about the *implications of the belief.*

THE CRITIQUE OF THE DOCTRINE OF THE INCARNATION

The critique of the doctrine of the Incarnation has mainly been the product of English or derivative American academic circles. Among the strongest voices I would include John Hick, Don Cupit, the contributors to *The Myth of God Incarnate* (the volume edited by Hick), and to a lesser extent John A. T. Robinson. Those who have been interested mostly in the *belief* in the Incarnation have been English "practical" theologians, defending the apparently high regard the Church of England has for the Incarnation; American theologians, particularly feminists and African-Americans; and some theologians worldwide who have been influenced by these and other liberation theologians. In England, Michael Ramsey is the foremost popular example. In America there is a wide range of examples, among them, James Cone, Letty Russell, Carter Heyward, Harvey Cox, Krister Stendahl, and Fredrica Harris Thompsett. C. S. Song and Desmond Tutu are primary examples of Asian and African voices building on incarnational themes.

I am arguing here that Anglicans have and ought to keep *an envisioning theology of the Incarnation*. To this end, it may be helpful to look at some twentieth-century theological comments on the Incarnation. From them we may find a greater sense of what this vocational accent will mean for Anglicans as we work and talk with other Christians. Because the doctrinal discussion assumes a more systematic approach, I will address it here. Modern understandings of *belief* in the Incarnation take place against the background of a pluralism that classical or reformed theology could hardly have imagined. These understandings really have to do with contemporary concerns for living out the implications of a belief in the Incarnation. (I will discuss these modern understandings as part of the next chapter.)

IS THE DOCTRINE OF THE INCARNATION AN EFFECTIVE DOCTRINE?

Several of the most influential theologians of the twentieth century have been merciless in their criticism of the *doctrine* of the Incarnation, and somewhat unkind to Anglicans, who are known to refer to it frequently. They are inheritors of the traditional Protestant understanding of justification by faith and the centrality of Atonement theology. Existential and historical confirmation of the great gulf between God and humanity was made obvious by the horrors of war and genocide. These played a major part in forming the reaction against the notion that God and humankind are somehow participants one with the other.

In *Theology of Culture*, Paul Tillich dismisses the doctrines related to the Incarnation in a few short lines:

> If we speak of the manifestation of the New Being in Christ, then we do not have to go into matters which involved the early church following its Greek philosophical need. Rightly for that period, but wrongly for us, there was need of a kind of divine-human-nature chemistry. What is understandable for people of our time, and what we can say today, is that we have a message of something which breaks the existential conflict and overcomes estrangement.[40]

In his *Systematic Theology*, Tillich went into greater depth, but drew the same conclusions. He conceded that the dogma concerning the Incarnation was necessary: "The christological dogma saved the church, but with very inadequate conceptual tools."[41] At the same time, he assigned the whole matter of christology, of which the doctrine of the Incarnation is a part, a subordinate place: "Christology," Tillich said, "is a function of soteriology." According to Tillich, that is, whatever we might say about the "universal significance of the event Jesus the Christ,"[42] it lies in the concern for salvation, not in the desire for union.

In *Christ the Center*, Dietrich Bonhoeffer, after offering a brilliant analysis of the doctrine of the Incarnation, finally says, "Strictly speaking, we should really talk, not about the Incarnation, but only about the Incarnate One. An interest in the incarnation raises the question, 'How?'"[43] The "how" too quickly returns to the formulation of doctrine. For this reason, Bonhoeffer was reported to be unwilling to begin his christology with a discussion of the Incarnation. E. H. Robertson, in the introduction to Bonhoeffer's *Christ the Center*, said, "Bonhoeffer refused to begin his lectures on Christology with what he called the 'alchemy of the incarnation.'" The classical discussion of the two natures seemed to him impertinent and certainly concerned with the wrong questions."[44]

The criticism of the doctrine, from Bonhoeffer's standpoint, is that it concerns itself with questions of *how* Jesus could be the Incarnation of God, rather than with *who* Jesus is. By moving the question from "Who do you say that I am?" to "How do you maintain that I can be both God and Man?" the rational and intellectual distance from Jesus is established. Bonhoeffer was profoundly concerned to make the question present-tense and turn it into a personal one. "A Christology which does not put at the beginning the statement, "God is only God *pro me*," "Christ is only Christ *pro me*," condemns itself."[45]

The issue is an existential one. From Bonhoeffer's standpoint, the *doctrine* fails the test of engagement at precisely a time when engagement is most important. It is not the doctrine of the Incarnation, but the Incarnate One who is central.

The basic criticism of the doctrine of the Incarnation is that it is ineffective: it cannot carry the weight it has been asked to bear. It either leads down wrong paths, or is internally flawed. It too easily takes us away from the cross of Christ and from the gulf between God and humankind, bridged by the atoning work of Christ.

THE DOCTRINE OF THE INCARNATION AS MYTH

John A. T. Robinson's book *Honest to God* links the question of the inefficacy of the doctrine of the Incarnation to the wider problem of demythologizing the faith. His hope was to raise these issues so that we might better understand Bonhoeffer's notion of a belief in Jesus beyond the boundaries of Enlightenment religion. Bishop Robinson has more often been misunderstood and simply viewed as a limited precursor to those concerned with demythologizing, in particular with the "Death of God" and the "Myth of God Incarnate" theologians.

This is a disservice to the work Robinson has done. He was fascinated with both Tillich and Bonhoeffer and saw them leading beyond the mythological dimensions of "God talk" to a more honest and profound depth. He popularized this in *Honest to God* and other works. His courage in calling us to consider the implications of religionless Christianity is remarkable. He gave us a wonderful statement of his own calling:

> I have tried simply to be honest, and to be open to certain "obstinate questionings" which speak to me of the need for what I called earlier a reluctant revolution. In it and through it, I am convinced, the fundamentals will remain, but only as we are prepared to sit loose to fundamentalisms of every kind. . . . [The] basic commitment to Christ may have been in the past—and may be for most of us still—buttressed and fortified by many lesser commitments—to a particular projection of God, a particular "myth" of the Incarnation, a particular code of morals, a particular pattern of religion. Without the buttresses it may look as if all would collapse. Nevertheless, we must beware of clinging to the buttresses instead of to Christ. And still more must we beware of insisting on the buttresses as the way to Christ.[46]

Bishop Robinson represented much of what Anglican openness can bring to theological debate, particularly as it applies to the stretching needed at the end of the life of a worldview. Nonetheless, when Hick's *The Myth of God Incarnate* appeared in 1977, only three references could be found to John Robinson, and only two of these references were to *Honest to God*. Interestingly, Bonhoeffer was not referenced at all and Tillich only in the retelling of a joke. The hint in Robinson's *Honest to God* to a "particular 'myth' of the Incarnation" was picked up by Robinson in his 1973 book, *The Human Face of God*; but by the time *The Myth of God Incarnate* appeared, even that hint was of no interest. Clearly the agenda had changed from demythologizing to discrediting and debunking myth.

Demythologizing the myths of the Incarnation involved a variety of tasks, some related to the birth narratives in the Gospels, some to the ancient questions of the nature of the person Jesus, some to the christologies that have over the years gained favor. Yet behind these questions, somewhat hidden, were the possibilities of a union between God and the creation. Continuing the tasks of demythologizing might well have led to renewed attention to the question of how we understand God to be related to the world. That task has been taken up, some twenty years later, by Marcus Borg and others who have tried to disentangle myths about God from their experience of God.

The mostly English "Myth of God Incarnate" debate is about the doctrine of the Incarnation, per se. That is, it is about what becomes, over time, the credal formulation. It suggests not only that the *doctrine* is a flawed one, but also that the Incarnation is not a biblically based, but a doctrinally determined, idea. The essays in *The Myth of God Incarnate* represent a last effort in the modern age to make doctrine amenable to reason rather than to belief.

Hick's own assessment of *The Myth of God Incarnate* is interesting,

> The generally polemical nature of the debates—and we authors of *The Myth* were as polemical as our critics— meant that a good deal of heat was generated along with the light. Nevertheless it seems clear in retrospect that this rather agitated phase of public discussion had to take place before a more calm and productive conversation could begin.[47]

That polemic had moved so far beyond what Robinson first spoke to in *Honest to God* that it is no wonder he was hardly referenced. Robinson had set out to show that Jesus should be considered, as Bonhoeffer suggested, "the man for others." Robinson felt that this belief, rather than the more abstracted and doctrinally determined model, was a beginning place for Christian faith in a world where we can only hope that God shares our suffering.

Robinson was able to address Bonhoeffer's question, "Who is Jesus Christ for me?" without relying on any doctrine of the Incarnation. Robinson described the Incarnate One this way:

> He was the complete expression, the Word, of God. Through him, as through no one else, God spoke and God acted: when one met him one was met—and saved and judged— by God. And it was to this conviction that the Apostles bore their witness. In this man, in his life, death and resurrection they had experienced God at work; and in the language of their day they confessed, like the centurion at the cross, "Truly this man was the Son of God" (Mark 15:39). Here was more than just a man: here was a window into God at work. For "God was in Christ reconciling the world to himself" (II Cor. 5:19).[48]

While Robinson saw Jesus as "a window into God at work," Michael Goulder, in his essay in *The Myth of God Incarnate*, calls Jesus "the man of universal destiny." In some ways he ends up in the same place as Robinson, with Jesus as "the complete expression, the Word, of God." Goulder says, "My faith is not in the unity of substance, but in the unity of activity of God and Jesus; *homopraxis*, if a Greek word is wanted, rather than *homoousia*."[49]

This seems to me, however, to be the exception in *The Myth of God Incarnate*. Much of what is argued shuts the door not only on further explorations of the doctrine of the Incarnation, but on talk about God as well. Robinson was right to begin with the question of the mythological structures of the language we use about God, and from there to be concerned about the specifics of the doctrine of the Incarnation. By the time he had suggested "a particular 'myth' of the Incarnation" he had already attempted to show how language about God might be translated into Tillich's "ground of being." Having addressed the former, however simply, Robinson was equipped to address the latter, but the path in English philosophical and theological thinking was headed another way. The "Myth of God Incarnate" debate finally seemed to lead to a dead end. When it included arguments against the philosophical formulation of a fourth-century doctrine, it was addressing something not very vital to most believers, although they might have stoutly defended the creed that resulted from this doctrine.

INCARNATION AS PRACTICE

Jesus was clearly known by his followers as someone in whom God's compassion was shown, and from whom God's will was to be gleaned. Within thirty years of his death the church was in a position to say that he was identified with God. The biblical record, Robinson contends, supports this: "The New Testament says that Jesus was the Word of God, it says that God was in Christ, it says that Jesus is the Son of God; but it does not say that Jesus was God, simply like that."[50]

It is this last that is problematic, that Jesus was God, "simply like that." If we could be content with "Jesus was [or is] the Word of God," that "God was in Christ," and that "Jesus is the Son of God," would that be enough? I believe it is enough. For many who have continued to find the Incarnation central to their religious understanding, the starting-point is precisely this—that the biblical witness and the belief of the church give us access to a powerful understanding of how God's incarnational presence in Christ prefigures our own vocation in the incarnation of God's compassion. Jesus is the example of the perfect practice of incarnational living.

The first sense of the early followers of Jesus seems to have been that Jesus was the Word or Wisdom of God. Word and Wisdom are at best human terms, involving a commerce between persons, a mutuality. Calling Jesus the Word or the Wisdom of God certainly set him apart, but it kept us in relation with him. Calling Jesus God, "simply like that," too quickly puts Jesus across that bridge with God, and we again find ourselves separated from God.

The three strands, then, of serious criticism of a theological environment in which a doctrine of the Incarnation is central, are these:

(1) Those who argue, like Tillich, that the Atonement, and not the Incarnation, is the central doctrine in a systematic theological approach.

(2) Those who argue, like Bonhoeffer and Robinson, that the Incarnation is distracting, since it leads us away from who Jesus Christ is, to how Jesus is the Christ.

(3) Those who argue, like Hick and the other contributors to *The Myth of God Incarnate,* that the doctrine of the Incarnation, and the church's understanding of its scriptural roots, are too much bound up with unwarranted mythology to be useful as theological constructs.

Against these arguments, Anglicans have on the whole countered with an insistence that the practice of incarnational living provides a viable counter to the criticisms about the theological environment and focus to which we seem to have such loyalty. It is to the practice of incarnational living that we now turn.

ENDNOTES

1. Throughout this discussion I want as much as possible to distinguish the Incarnation—a belief, growing from faith, affirming that God was in Jesus the Christ—from the doctrine of the Incarnation, a formulation of a belief about the Incarnation, and a complex intellectual construct.

2. Morgan, *Agenda for Anglicans,* 32; citing Einer Molland, *Christendom* (1959), 148.

3. U. Holmes, *What Is Anglicanism?* 27–29.

4. Ramsey, *The Anglican Spirit,* 21–22.

5. Ibid., 30. See 30–31 for Ramsey's wider statement concerning the appeal to reason.

6. Ibid., 87–88.

7. Ibid., 89–90.

8. U. Holmes, ibid., 30.

9. John 8:32b ("the truth will make you free") is the motto. in Greek on the Anglican Communion's emblem, the Compass Rose.

10. U. Holmes, ibid., 5.

11. Ramsey, ibid., 19.

12. Marshall, *The Anglican Church Today and Tomorrow,* 133–34; citing *The Lambeth Conference 1968* (SPCK and Seabury Press, 1968), 140–41.

13. Allchin, *Participation in God,* 1–2, speaks to this possibility.

14. *Lux Mundi*, the famous collection of late-nineteenth-century Anglican essays edited by Charles Gore, was subtitled *A Series of Studies in the Religion of the Incarnation*, by which was meant not the doctrine, but the belief behind the doctrine.

15. The Book of Common Prayer (1979), 13.

16. I am not suggesting that the belief in the Atonement is problematic, only that the doctrines that grew up around it in the late Middle Ages are problematic.

17. Borg, *Meeting Jesus Again for the First Time*, 46–68.

18. J. R. Illingworth, "The Incarnation and Development," in Gore, ed., *Lux Mundi*, 152–53, makes a strong argument that the reformers were "so occupied with what is now called Soteriology that. . .the religion of the Incarnation was narrowed into the religion of the Atonement."

19. Borg, ibid., 50–58.

20. See 1 Cor. 1:23.

21. Crossan, *The Essential Jesus*, 1–25.

22. H. U. von Balthasar, intro. to Irenaeus, *The Scandal of the Incarnation*, 53.

23. Ibid., 54; citing *Against the Heresies* III:20:2; preface to Book V.

24. Von Balthasar, ibid., 39.

25. Ibid., 76.

26. Ibid., 82.

27. Allchin, *Participation in God*, 1. Note that this is a somewhat different translation of the line in *De incarnatione verbi Dei* given by von Balthasar (Irenaeus, *The Scandal of the Incarnation*, 93) as, "He, indeed, assumed humanity that we might become God." Phrased this way, the translation more clearly relates to Irenaeus's formula, "He became what we are in order to make us what He is."

28. Allchin, ibid.

29. The Book of Common Prayer, 855.

30. I am indebted to Fredrica Harris Thompsett for her lecture notes on "Renewing Incarnational Theology" for a perspective on Hooker in the wider context of Anglican thought on the Incarnation.

31. Allchin, ibid., 9; citing Hooker, *Laws of Ecclesiastical Polity* I.11.2, in *Works*, ed. John Keble (1836), vol. I.

32. Allchin, ibid., 69.

33. Ibid., 77.

34. Harrison, ed., *The First and Second Prayer Books of Edward VI*, 390.

35. Ibid., 382.

36. Richard Hooker, *Laws of Ecclesiastical Polity*, in Hill, ed., *Works*, V.50.3.

37. Ibid., V.50.3.

38. Ibid., V.56.7, emphasis added.

39. Ibid., V.5.4.

40. Tillich, *Theology of Culture*, 211–12.

41. Tillich, *Systematic Theology*, 2:140.

42. Ibid., 2:150. This is the rubric under which Tillich examines the whole question of the uniqueness of Jesus Christ.

43. Bonhoeffer, *Christ the Center*, 109.

44. E. H. Robertson, intro. to Bonhoeffer, ibid., 21.

45. Ibid., 48.

46. Robinson, *Honest to God*, 140–41.

47. Hick, *The Metaphor of God Incarnate*, 2–3.

48. Robinson, ibid., 71.

49. Michael Goulder, "Jesus, the Man of Universal Destiny," in Hick, ed., *The Myth of God Incarnate*, 62.

50. Robinson, ibid., 70.

CHAPTER 4

ENGAGEMENT WITH THE WORLD
THE PRACTICE OF INCARNATIONAL LIVING

I am convinced that Anglicans have something of value to contribute to the larger community of Christians. We structure our common life as a *koinonia*. We have developed a theological method grounded in our experience of the Incarnation. We have learned to live provisionally. These are skills that will be of great value to Christians in societies that are increasingly post-modern and post-Christian. These skills are even more important in a pluralistic global community, in which the triumphalism of Christendom is an insult and modernity as presented in the west is viewed as evil. Within the Christian community Anglicans can practice a faith that liberates the believer from both the dualisms of modernity and from the incrustations of Christendom. It is sometimes hard for us to see this as a possibility.

THE GOSPEL THAT LIBERATES

A remarkable number of people all over the world are convinced that the gospel liberates. Many of them believe the good news of God in Christ is immediately and incarnationally available, and that it comes in forms not determined by prior experience, but by immediate need.

Both in America and in the rest of the world there are movements and people who understand the *belief* in the Incarnation to be liberating. That liberation is known in practice—in living out the implications of the Incarnation. I have chosen to speak of this practice as that of "incarnational living." The testimony to this liberating practice and belief in the Incarnation takes many forms. I want to explore four of them briefly, since I believe they have much to tell us, as Anglicans, about the vocational implications of our belief in the Incarnation.

The liberation these movements speak to begins always as liberation *from* one or another restriction on the power of the Incarnation. And the great liberation *for* the presence of God in creation is experienced in the rejection of limitation. This should not surprise us, for we say the Magnificat (the Song of Mary), deeply conscious of the close connection between liberation *from*, and liberation *for:* "He has cast down the mighty from their thrones, and has lifted up the lowly. He has filled the hungry with good things, and the rich he has sent away empty." The initial shock of such liberation needs to be faced squarely. Unless the Incarnation is liberated from the assumed picture of Jesus as the Incarnate One, the most likely candidates for the practice of incarnational living are held captive by an image. So I want to look at the notion that the Incarnation needs to be freed from the notions that it is a unique event, and that the Incarnate One is *white, male*, or *western*.

The careful reader will note that many of those I refer to in this chapter are not Anglicans. I am drawing on the work of contemporary theologians of many traditions and locations. I do so because I believe these theologians point out elements of a liberating gospel that we ought to take seriously. I also believe that Anglicans already practice their faith in ways that are open to *liberation from* and *liberation for*. We have always been informed by theologians from the rest of the Christian community, and rather than seeing that as a problem, we ought to rejoice in the gifts they bring us.

INCARNATION FREED FROM UNIQUENESS

The first freedom, the freedom from uniqueness, is of course at the center, for it is what finally frees us to be God's presence in our own day and to become the body of Christ. I believe the prevailing understanding of the uniqueness of Jesus as the Christ has made it increasingly difficult to understand our mission in relation to his or to think of ourselves as participants in the Incarnation.

"Everyone always knows that [in interfaith dialogue] the question of who Jesus was and is, and what he means today, will inevitably appear,"[1] says Harvey Cox. In response Christians often make a claim for the uniqueness of Christ and the exclusive truth of the Christian witness. We have often wanted to limit the use of incarnational motifs and theologies to specific assertions about Jesus as the Christ, and to no other person or aspect of creation. When Christians engage other faiths, that sense of uniqueness is quite clearly present. It is often a difficult subject.

As the beginning of a program of engagement with people of other faiths, Cox has outlined in his book *Many Mansions* the basic features of a "hospitable" understanding of the Incarnation.[2] These are not the full-blown elements of a *doctrine*, but elements of belief:

(1) Jesus is the particularity, the specific of our faith: the incarnation of God;

(2) Jesus comes to establish God's reign, in which justice and compassion are essential;

(3) Jesus is open to what is beyond doctrine and words; and

(4) Jesus is open to God as present in others.

This picture of the Incarnate One grows from a sense of specificity, of particularity, in which it is the Jesus *of history* who is central rather than the *Christ of faith*. Cox argues that the Jesus of the Gospels is more open to people of other faiths than is the Christ known by faith, mediated by the church.

Krister Stendahl makes a similar argument. Like Cox he has expressed great concern that Christians come to interfaith dialogue with a sense of humility that grows from acknowledging the pluralism that exists. The first element of that humility is to recognize that "universalism" is the ultimate arrogance in the realm of religion. It is by definition unavoidably a "spiritual colonialism, a spiritual imperialism."[3]

Letty Russell, in *Church in the Round: Feminists' Interpretation of the Church*, expresses much the same thing. She states,

> To universalize our very concrete and particular faith is a form of imperialism over people of other faiths and ideologies. In humility we can witness to the faith that God has indeed begun the New Creation in Christ, and that for us this is the message of salvation, but still look forward to God's fulfillment of the promise of salvation and liberation for all.[4]

And yet, given the particularity of Jesus as a historical event, and the clear implications of that for the early church—that he indeed is the Messiah and the Incarnate God—how can we not claim uniqueness? Stendahl poses the question this way: "I ask myself: how to sing my song to Jesus with abandon without telling negative stories about others?"[5] His answer acknowledges both the particularity of the Jesus event for Christians and the particularity of the people of Jesus Christ. The uniqueness of Jesus, as the Son of God, is a uniqueness *for us as Christians.* The Jews, says Stendahl, saw themselves a peculiar people, but not the only people worthy of God's grace. They were and are a minority people. So it should be for Christians: we should see ourselves as a peculiar, minority people.[6]

This approach makes the particularity of Jesus and the belief in Jesus as the Incarnation of God a gift to the whole world, known and celebrated by a peculiar people. It does not necessarily assume the exclusive and triumphalist conclusion that outside belief in Jesus there is no salvation. Stendahl disarms one of the basic texts for this triumphalism—"for there is no other name under heaven given among human beings, whereby we must be saved" (Acts 4:12)—by noting that this is Peter's praise of God rather than his exclusion of others.[7]

Both Cox and Stendahl clearly understand that Christians must begin at the beginning: with Jesus, in his full particularity. As believers, they share the special and distinctive understanding of Jesus as the incarnational presence of God. Yet neither contends that this belief excludes the possibilities that God is present for others in other ways, or that Jesus thought otherwise. What they have both noted is that the Incarnation need not lead to exclusivist claims.

Recent biblical scholarship has provided both of these writers with invaluable tools to aid them in their task. Until perhaps the mid-1970s,

access to the Jesus of history was severely limited by the failed results
of the earlier search for the historical Jesus. Only when new tools of
scholarship, new texts, and new methods of analysis arose was there be
any sense that perhaps the Jesus of history was available, *in at least
some of his particularities*. Only then did there begin to be a turning
from christologies that primarily spoke of the Christ of faith and the
beliefs of the early church, to christologies that referred to the Jesus of
history and to the reaffirmed sayings and actions of Jesus. With access
to something of the historical Jesus it is more easily possible to reassess
Resurrection and Atonement motifs and find greater value in those of
Incarnation and compassion.

The rediscovery of the historical Jesus is immensely important to
Anglican thought and practice precisely because the Incarnation is a
concrete matter. Incarnational theology and practice are grounded in
there being at least this one example of God's presence among us,
whose peculiarities are available to us.

Dietrich Bonhoeffer, like Cox, was aware that, "Everyone always
knows that the question of who Jesus was and is, and what he means
today, will inevitably appear."[8] For Bonhoeffer, the assertion of the pre-
eminence of the historical Jesus in any discussion of Jesus Christ was
clear:

> The Christological question, of its very nature, must be
> addressed to the whole Christ, the one Christ. This whole
> Christ is the historical Jesus who can never in any way be
> divorced from his work. He is asked and he replies as the
> one who is himself his work. But Christology primarily
> seeks his being and not his action. To put it in abstract
> terms: the subject of Christology is the personal structure of
> being of the whole, historical Jesus Christ.

Bonhoeffer insisted on taking the historical Jesus seriously, in spite
of the difficulties presented by the failure of historical criticism. This
grew from the clarity of his belief that a Christ separated from the Jesus
of history was not Jesus Christ at all. "Dogmatics needs to be certain of
the historicity of Jesus Christ, i.e., of the identity of the Christ of
preaching with the Jesus of history."[9]

Harvey Cox suggests that, "The most nettlesome dilemma hinder-
ing interreligious dialogue is the very ancient one of how to balance the

universal and the particular."[10] Parallel to that is the problem of the transcendent and the immanent. The claim that Jesus is God links the two, the universal and the particular, the transcendent and the immanent, in a unique way, is a claim that as believers we find a source of wonder and joy. At the same time, unless we understand that uniqueness as uniqueness *for us,* as something God has given *us* to see, we can easily slip into arrogance. That which is unique for us does not make all other religious solutions to connecting human particularity and the transcendent false or inadequate.

Peter Berger has attempted to approach the same problem—that of our *specific* particularity in relation to the transcendent—in his book *A Far Glory.* He says,

"Reality is haunted by the otherness which lurks behind the fragile structures of everyday life. . . .From time to time we catch glimpses of transcendent reality as the business of living is interrupted or put in question for one reason or another. And occasionally, rarely, the other breaks into our world in manifestations of dazzling, overwhelming brilliance."[11]

For Christians, such a manifestation "of dazzling, overwhelming brilliance" is seen in Jesus. But what was true in the early church and affirmed in the creeds, Berger argues, is no longer true.

> We do have a problem of belief, and it not only raises the question of why we should believe in God but why we should believe in *this* God. There are others, after all, and today they are made available in an unprecedented way through the religious supermarket of modern pluralism.[12]

Berger warns us of the cost of openness. The problems of the transcendent/universal and the immanent/particular will confront and challenge our beliefs. Suddenly there are too many choices. Cultural censorship, imposed or accidental, keeps the choices limited. But when pluralism is available within a culture, the possibility arises that the uniqueness of a particular manifestation of God (as for example in Jesus Christ) is effectively compromised and undercut.

What I believe Cox and Stendahl have laid out for us is the possibility that the Jesus of the Gospels has called us to an openness to other manifestations of God's presence in the world. They argue that the

Incarnation, as experienced, supports that openness. What Berger does is clearly state the price.

For Anglicans this widening application of the notion of Incarnation means that the focus on the God "made manifest" frees the notion itself from the bondage to uniqueness. It is possible to believe that Jesus Christ is the Incarnation of God, to affirm that this is so, and at the same time to believe that God's manifestation of self is a matter of God's hospitality to humankind. Incarnational living becomes a way of expressing the particularities of our profound beliefs concerning Jesus the Christ and our continued confidence that God's manifestation of self occurs in many ways.

INCARNATION FREED FROM BEING WHITE

Until the middle of the twentieth century, the majority of the world's Anglicans were white and lived in one of very few "western" or "northern" countries. While that did not mean that being white was a dominant category of self-understanding for all those many Anglicans, it did mean that their understanding of the world was hedged about with experiences quite different from those of other people. Their experience of Jesus, of the faith, and of the church was likewise formed in this context.

For almost all of Anglican history, England and the English language have determined Anglican sensibilities. This meant that Anglicans were mostly white. And for them, so was Jesus. But there is an emerging world culture for Anglicanism, one that will force us to deal squarely with God's presence cast in other than white form. That challenge may be too great for the Anglican Communion. However, there is every hope that the power of that mutuality that was enfleshed in Jesus can be exhibited anew as we move beyond what has been given to what is given now in the richness of our *koinonia*. I believe that the Anglican Communion has a vocation to press beyond a Western European experience of Jesus the Christ to embrace, in all its churches, an image of the Incarnation that is no longer white.

It is not at all clear that we will be able to do so. In this instance, the good news begins by liberation from being white. That is not good news to those who up to this time have determined the agenda of mission, both domestic and foreign. It is striking to note that many hospitals and schools have been founded and supported by Anglicans, but that very few liberation movements have even been encouraged. The Jesus who heals and teaches may look a bit like the doctor sent to staff the hospital or the teacher sent to teach. The Jesus who liberates is always finally to be numbered among the oppressed. His identity will, more often than not, be black or brown or yellow or red.

Mission agencies in the traditional "sending" Anglican churches have been struggling with how to move beyond the Incarnation as White for some time. For a short period it appeared that the "sending" churches would take the idea of Mutual Responsibility and Interdependence (MRI) to heart. From the time of its inception at the Anglican Congress in Toronto in 1963, the idea of MRI has challenged the churches of the Anglican Communion to stop thinking of the incarnational presence of the Christ as flowing from "sending" to "receiving" churches. That challenge was taken on for several years. The official mission sending agencies have continued to endorse its principles. But it has become more and more apparent that members of the "sending" churches continue to see themselves as "bringing Christ" to "receiving" churches. For example, there is an obstinate refusal by many members of the Episcopal Church to recognize that sending American (and mostly white) missionaries to the Philippines and supporting over two hundred Filipino clergy in mission in the Philippines are both elements of the missionary enterprise, both activities of incarnational practice. It is difficult not to see this as a failure to understand the Incarnation as liberated from being exclusively white.

"From the outset," says James Cone, "the Gospels wish to convey that the Jesus story is not simply a story about a good man who met an unfortunate fate. Rather, in Jesus God is at work, telling his story and disclosing the divine plan of salvation."[13]

> Jesus understood his person and work as the inauguration of the new age, which is identical with freedom for the oppressed and health for the sick. Accordingly, any understanding of the Kingdom in Jesus' teaching that fails to make the poor and their liberation its point of departure is a contradiction of Jesus' presence.[14]

Cone asks in *God of the Oppressed* the question raised by Bonhoeffer: "Who is Jesus Christ for us today?" His answer is a remarkable statement of a christology that encompasses the past, present, and future. Cone makes the point that christology always takes place in a social context, but it always relies on the foundational work presented in the Bible, in which are provided the source testimonies.

> The variety of these testimonies enriches our perception of Christ while reminding us that words cannot capture him. The Gospel of Mark speaks of him as the Son of God, while John's Gospel says that he is "the offspring of God himself," "the Word [that] became flesh to well among us." (John 1:13–14)[15]

For Cone, it is precisely because Jesus is understood to be doing the work of God—because he is witnessed to as God among us—that he is seen as a touchstone for liberation. Cone challenges the world of white theology with the image of the Black Christ. The Black Christ melds together (1) the historical Jesus, who incarnated God's presence; (2) the suffering Christ of the present, identified with the oppressed; and (3) the Christ of the future, whose work is judgment and release.

Jesus is identified with the poor and the oppressed through suffering.[16] Cone clearly understands this dynamic clearly: "His presence with the poor today is not docetic; but like yesterday, today also he takes the pain of the poor upon himself and bears it for them."[17] This echoes Bonhoeffer, who in *Christ the Center* writes of humiliation and exaltation as "the way God exists as man."[18] He understands suffering to be central to the force of the claim that the historical Jesus is in fact God with us and for us. It is that identification that for Cone brings the particularity of the historical Jesus into focus in the present and identifies it as the source of liberation for the oppressed.

> I contend that there is no universalism that is not particular. . . .My point is that God came, and continues to come, to those who are poor and helpless, for the purpose of setting them free. . . .The "blackness of Christ," therefore, is not simply a statement about skin color, but rather the transcendent affirmation that God has not ever, no not ever, left the oppressed alone in the struggle. He was with them in Pharaoh's Egypt, is with them in America, Africa and Latin

America, and will come in the end of time to consummate
fully their human freedom.[19]

Again we see the insistence on the particularity of the Incarnation
of the Christ in the present. The presence of God in Christ, if seen only
as a universal statement of doctrine, can on the one hand lead to a
Christian triumphalism, and on the other hand to a lessening of focus
on the oppressed. The Incarnation is meaningless unless its present-
tense form is particularized in some way in a people, and particularly
in the poor. Cone finally says,

> It seems clear that the overwhelming weight of biblical
> teaching, especially the prophetic tradition in which Jesus
> stood unambiguously, is upon God's unqualified identifica-
> tion with the poor precisely because they are poor. The
> kingdom of God is for the helpless, because they have no
> security in this world.[20]

The belief in the Incarnation carries with it great power, for it
opens the possibility that what was true of Jesus can be true of you and
me, and of the whole creation. If the identity of Jesus as human is with
the oppressed and the suffering, then the Divinity also is so identified.

Jesus as the Incarnation of God is not white, not so much as a matter of color, although indeed that is no doubt true as well. Jesus is freed
from being white precisely because God's manifestation of self is freed
from being a matter of class, caste, race, sex or any other limiting factor. The Incarnation, and therefore the practice of incarnational living,
is freed from identification with this or that standard. "The saints of
God," says the song, "are just folk like me," but they are *not only* like
me. Incarnational living requires that we see God's manifestation and
incarnation of self in a much wider range of possibilities than our limitations could imagine. Otherwise, the historical Jesus rapidly becomes
the Jesus of my own limited vision. He becomes less God present for
the poor, and more God present for the anxious.

INCARNATION FREED FROM THE MALE

It is surprising just how *male* the Incarnation is and has been. The
enfleshment of God in Jesus was clearly an incarnation as a *male*
Palestinian peasant almost two thousand years ago. That fact has had

far-ranging influence—far, I believe, out of proportion to the sort of fact it is. For most of Anglican practice it has meant that leadership within the church has also been male. The notion—that the particulars of God's Incarnation dictate that only men be at the "head"—has been with us a long time. Only in this century has there been any significant effort to liberate the Incarnation from being male.

Incarnational thinking is central to Anglican practice. But given this strange equation of Incarnation with the male, is the accent on the Incarnation at all useful to feminists who are also Anglican? Carter Heyward answered that in an essay titled, "Can Anglicans be Feminist Liberation Theologians and Still be 'Anglican'?: An Essay on an Improbable Identity." The shorter version of this is in her book *Speaking of Christ* and is the title essay.[21] Her response is, Yes, but only with difficulty! The "yes" is clear:

> The focus, albeit controversial, in modern Anglicanism on the incarnational character of the whole creation testifies to how seriously Anglicans may take the profoundly sacramental constitution of our world. Nowhere is this significant emphasis any more apparent than in the contemporary efforts of feminist liberation theologians to offer images of incarnation that do justice to the whole earth and its inhabitants, not merely to the christological preserves of church fathers.[22]

The "no" is also there. The "christological preserves of church fathers" not only made the Incarnation a mystery best pursued by those with knowledge (i.e., men of privilege—for example, those with access to education) but totally unique, and therefore *outside* the purview of those seeking liberation or wholeness (i.e., the poor and oppressed). The classical formulation is built on a dualism—Bonhoeffer calls this "negative" christology—a dualism consisting of the good God and the alienated or bad world. In the perverted understanding of the Adam and Eve story, this becomes the dualism between the good natural man and the evil natural woman. The solution, of course, was seen in the Atonement, and the instrument for this atonement was male, the crucified God, Jesus Christ.

> The problem with this scenario is twofold: In worshipping Jesus as *the* Christ, *the* Son, *the* Savior, we close our eyes to

the possibility of actually seeing that the sacred liberating Spirit is *as* incarnate here and now among us as She was in Jesus of Nazareth. We cannot recognize that redemption is an ongoing process which was neither begun nor completed, historically, in the life, death, and resurrection of Jesus. Reflecting this same tendency is the similarly exclusivist assumption that Christians are *the* people with *the* way, *the* truth, and *the* life. Thus as Christians, we learn to recognize ourselves primarily as *unlike* "the world," "pagans," "heretics," Jews. . . .[23]

Both Heyward and Cox agree that there is a growing need to be open "to the possibility of actually seeing that the sacred liberating Spirit is *as* incarnate here and now among us as She was in Jesus of Nazareth."[24] Most interestingly, Heyward echoes Michael Goulder's notion of *homopraxis*[25] in her suggestion that, "what has been missing in the dominant structures of Christian faith and discourse has been a *praxis of relational particularity and cooperation.*"[26]

Fredrica Harris Thompsett, speaking as a feminist and as an Anglican historian and theologian, also takes up the theme of "a praxis of relational particularity and cooperation." She sees the stress on the Incarnation as central to the transformation of theology and the widening of the "hospitality" of the church. About the Incarnation she says,

> In a world undergoing major shifts, the Incarnation still holds power to create change, to inspire meaning, to reveal and challenge today's paradigms. I believe two things will begin to happen when we seek to understand human life in light of the images and insights of the Incarnation. We will be open to learning theology anew, seeking fuller understanding of God, humanity, and creation, and we will also discover timeless resources for interpreting today's contexts and crises.[27]

For Thompsett, this process is tied to hospitality, an openness to others. In trying to understand ourselves in the light of the Incarnation, she asks,

> How do we continue our search for religious enlightenment living, as Christians do, among peoples of many and of no religions? Can we begin to define our terms in ways that directly increase our abilities to communicate across boundaries that seem to set us apart from others?[28]

Thompsett is concerned that we be clear about what we bring to the table when we bring an incarnational faith. She states,

> It is important to begin theological reflection on the Incarnation by considering what it reveals about God. For although we may be more likely to consider what this doctrine implies for the human condition, the story of incarnation is first of all a statement about God's nature. Images of God revealed in the incarnation are those of an intimately engaged, concrete, and "worldly" deity. This is a God with a remarkable readiness to take on the conditions of mortal life, including vulnerability, responsibility, and risk. . . .This is an active God who transforms reality by embracing it. . . .The Incarnation also reveals a God with sure commitment to humankind.[29]

It is this openness in the Incarnation, by which God is ready "to take on the conditions of mortal life" that seems to be attractive to both Heyward and Thompsett. Both see Jesus as the sign and image of a God willing to engage the universe and particular people in their struggles for liberation. Heyward's contention is that "The christological task of Christian feminism is to move the foundations of Christology from the ontology of dualistic opposition toward the ethics of justice-making. This happens only in a praxis of relational particularity and cooperation."[30]

Thompsett sees the matter of praxis from another quarter when she notes how "the enfleshed nature of human intimacy has long challenged and troubled theologians," and asks, "Does the relational mutuality embodied in the doctrine of the Incarnation suggest more affirming patterns for our most intimate relationships?[31]

What these two Anglican, feminist liberation theologians are doing, it seems, is taking the matter of belief out of the context of doctrine, and opening it again to matters of experience. The question is not, "What is the relation between God the transcendent and Jesus the finite?" Rather, the question is, "What is the relation between *God the Source* and *all that is,* such that Jesus and you and I—and indeed all of creation—have a part in incarnating God's love?" In that context we then can ask the question asked by Bonhoeffer, "Who is Jesus Christ for me [today]?" The wider question of God's incarnational desire deserves the attention that Christians have always given to the specific willingness of God to give his only Son.

We must also note here that it is with the Anglican feminists that incarnational thinking begins to be linked with concepts such as "relational mutuality," "cooperation," and "hospitality." These will be increasingly important implications of incarnational thinking as Anglicans begin to look at the vocational implications of an incarnational stance.

INCARNATION FREED FROM THE WEST

Some years ago I visited an Ethiopian Orthodox parish church in Addis Ababa. The parish was having a liturgical gathering drawing many worshipers from churches in the area. There in a large dusty compound a whole variety of activities were taking place. In one part of the nave of the church a choir of elderly women was chanting; in the portico across from the church proper a priest or deacon was reading the Gospel; in another part of the compound two country priests were preaching. At the entry to the compound there were books and religious items for sale. The images, smells, sounds, actions, all were quite strange to me. I knew I was in the midst of a Christian community, but it was unlike any I had ever experienced. I was not in the west anymore. The practice and life of this community was older than anything growing out of the churches of Europe. I knew that God was incarnated there, just as God is incarnated everywhere the faithful gather. I understood that to experience God incarnate is to experience God in context. But understanding that was not enough. For me to that visit opened my eyes to a deeper sensibility. For me to experience the presence of God in that church in Addis Ababa made me realize that the Incarnation must be freed from the west.

Anglicans the world over recognize just how much we are formed by the body of Christ as it found incarnational form in England. Most particularly our sense of good and appropriate public or "common" prayer rests on the experiences of Western European Christianity molded in a particular way in England. Less clearly recognized is the extent to which our understanding of the primacy of scripture grows from the particular circumstances of the Reformation—a western phenomenon. Both Bible and Prayer Book as we have them are part of the western kit bag. What would it mean for the Incarnation to be freed from the west? What would constitute the kit bag elsewhere?

Archbishop Tutu, in his presentation defending the work of the South African Council of Churches (SACC) to the Eloff Commission on Sept. 1, 1982, began by making it clear that the SACC was being called to judgment precisely because it was Christian. He took the opportunity to instruct the commissioners on what that meant.

> The Bible describes God as creating the universe to be a cosmos and not a chaos, a cosmos in which harmony, unity, order, fellowship, communion, peace and justice would reign and that this divine intention was disturbed by sin. The result was disunity, alienation, disorder, chaos, enmity, separation, and that in the face of this God then sent His Son to restore that primordial harmony to effect reconciliation. By becoming a real human being through Jesus Christ, God showed that He took the whole of human history and the whole of human life seriously.[32]

The religion of Incarnation was central to this defense, because if God showed that he took humanity "seriously," then so must we. "The Incarnation means that we must take all human life seriously, body, mind and spirit."[33] The political dimensions of the identification of our actions with the Incarnation are powerful and, of course, astounding, to those who have not experienced the Incarnation as liberating.

> I will soon show that the central work of Jesus was to effect reconciliation between God and us and also between man and man. Consequently from a theological and scriptural base, I will demonstrate that apartheid, separate development or whatever it is called is evil, totally and without remainder, that it is unchristian and unbiblical.[34]

There are numerous examples of other Anglican theologians from the Southern Hemisphere who have understood incarnational thinking, believing, or theology as the framework for involvement by the church in the world for the tasks of contextualization. In doing so, they have built on the sense, well understood by Anglicans, that God, as the Creator and Source of all, is "goodness" (to use Hooker's term). We are caught, as Archbishop Tutu says, in that "redeeming, reconciling, forgiving, welcoming love."[35]

In much of the world, and more and more in the west, that love is termed *compassion*. Compassion links the particularity of context to the particularity of Jesus as the Incarnation of God. C. S. Song, closing out a remarkable chapter titled "The Mandate of Heaven" in his book *The Compassionate God*, remarks,

> The Spirit of God does work in diverse and strange ways. Its manifestation in various lands and among different peoples cannot always be predicted. That is why we as Christians must be alert if we want to see God's signals in the lives of other peoples, to understand God's signs in the history of other nations, and to decipher God's will in the struggle of suffering persons outside the familiar domain of Christianity.[36]

He proposes that Christians undertake "transpositional theology," because "theology has already become transposed from its home in the West to other parts of the world."[37] In that transposition certain questions arise and certain roadblocks are discovered. "One of the roadblocks. . .is the centrism with which traditional theology is accustomed to view the history of Israel and the history of Christianity."[38] The end result of removing that roadblock is to "clear the road for the third step: our journey into movements of nations and peoples in Asia that may give us some clues to the ways of God in that vast portion of the world outside the Judeo-Christian traditions."[39]

From the first pages of this important work Song concerns himself with the Incarnation. Almost at once he draws on a quite different understanding of theological discourse when he comments at length on *art objects* as a means of theological expression. About the "Brown Madonna" by Galo Ocampo, he says,

> In fact the painting conveys the ultimate meaning of the incarnation: God was in Christ becoming one of us. Above all, both the Madonna and the Child are completely Asian, including their noses, which are pointedly flat. Transposition from the point-nosed Christ to the flat-nosed Christ has taken place.[40]

The dynamics of *transposition* are understood by Song to be central to an incarnational faith, and a great risk to culturally bound Christian doctrine:

> The gospel, when transposed from its biblical world to other cultural worlds, undergoes change itself as well as causing those other worlds to change. . . .In our mission and theology,

we have constantly underestimated this enormous changeability of the gospel. But it is this changeability that makes
the gospel what it is—the good news that God loves and
saves people. How can the gospel not be changeable? The
heart of the gospel is that God comes to the world. God
becomes flesh in humanity, is incarnate in Jesus Christ and
through him in us all.[41]

The risk, of course for those who are "timid," is the "fear
that we may lose sight of God in the temples of other believers. We are not sure whether we can hold onto God in the
sea of humanity that crowds the streets of Hong Kong."[42]

Song challenges believers in the Incarnation of God in Jesus Christ to
see the incarnation in new ways: on the one hand, open to Jesus as Asian
or Black or Woman; on the other hand, open to God's manifestation in
other religions and peoples. These two sides reveal some of the reason for
the book's title, *The Compassionate God*. Compassion means God coming
as Jesus among *us*, a specific people, in a form with which we can identify. Compassion also means God manifesting God's self among a people in
ways that are specific to their own history, in a form that Jesus, as God's
incarnation, could engage. Transposition is thus a dynamic in the compassionate engagement of God with the whole of creation.

Song challenges our fears of pluralism, saying,

As Christians we bear witness to God's extension and pene-
tration into humanity in the person of Jesus Christ. . . .If
God has made such an extension to the world, is there any
reason why we should be afraid of extending ourselves in
our faith and theology? Is there any reason why Christianity
should remain a one-size religion, Christian theology a one-
size system of beliefs, and we Christians one-size religious
beings?[43]

The belief in the Incarnation is at the core of this challenge, and at
the same time it is that belief that makes the challenge such a great
one. Just as with black and feminist theologies, this sort of Asian theology liberates precisely insofar as it takes Incarnation seriously for
people often excluded in image and person from engagement with the
faith. The compassion of the "Compassionate God" is in the openness
and freedom God brings even to those people who have received the
good news from oppressors.

ANGLICANS AND INCARNATION IN A PLURALISTIC WORLD

I suggested in the last chapter that the Anglican stress on Incarnation presents an important theological corrective to Atonement theology. I believe it is central to our vocation as Anglicans, thus the time given to it in this work. This corrective must wrestle with the objection, sometimes raised by Anglicans and often by our critics, that the *doctrine* of the Incarnation is difficult to defend as a doctrine. While true, this is something of a dead end, for we are less often motivated by doctrine and more often by experience and the beliefs that grow from experience. Those most interested in the *belief* in the Incarnation seem to be those who have been in one way or another excluded from the theological debate about the doctrine, or for whom the exclusive claims of Christianity have seemed increasingly absurd. They draw some comfort from those who criticize the doctrine *qua* doctrine. But in all honesty, there is little to indicate that they have much interest in the academic evolution of that debate.

Those of other cultures, those who engage other faiths with respect, and those seeking liberation from oppression, find a common ground in incarnational *models* that open out to new ways to meet God in the world. Incarnational thinking leads them beyond the enlightenment paradigm. As a result, the theological explorations change in form: they are no longer stated in rationalist or epistemological terms, they are stated in ethical-justice terms and in cultural context. As Bonhoeffer suggests, it is no longer a matter of "how" but of "who." When what is profoundly needed is a sense of God's compassionate justice in the world, we want to know who Jesus is for our world, not abstractly how God could be human.

Having something of the hints of what a belief in the Incarnation would look like freed from the burdens of uniqueness, of being white, male or western, I would suggest a definition of Incarnation as a practical belief:

The Incarnation is primarily a belief that involves compassion—God's compassion toward the whole of creation, and the possibility of our "transposition" of that compassion from one of us to another in ways that change us all more into God's incarnate daughters and sons.

We also need to extend the metaphor of the Incarnation so that the insights gained, and the faith expressed, in knowing Jesus as the Incarnation of God are not lost when we look at all of God's creation. In *Courageous Incarnation,* Fredrica Harris Thompsett quotes Sallie McFague: "We can speak of God's incarnation in two ways: first, creation as a whole (God's body) is a sacrament or sign of the presence of God, and second, human beings. . .are sacraments or signs of God the lover."[44] Thompsett then comments, "Both images—the incarnation of creation and the more familiar incarnation of God in Christ dwelling among us—express the theme of human interdependence with God's purpose."[45]

So, a second observation:

Incarnational believing and thinking is open-ended, and yet for Christians it is grounded in Jesus. The particularity of Jesus as the Incarnation is never lost on those who love him, even when who he is, as God Incarnate, becomes understood as "first fruits" of what, in compassion, we must come to see in ourselves, in all people, and indeed in the universe itself.

I am struck, too, with the strong sense that the pluralism, which, in previous theological generations was examined as a characteristic *within* western Christian society, is now seen as the experience of people worldwide. Pluralism may at one time have been about Methodists and Lutherans and Episcopalians in the same community. Now pluralism is an experience of world cultures and world culture.

The theologies that are arising in minority or oppressed communities bearing the title "liberation" are always related to worldwide phenomena and concerns. The analysis they bring consistently calls for an openness to what God is doing in a world larger than that provided by the worldview of oppressor peoples.

What does the future of Jesus the Incarnation of God look like? In cultures not part of the Judeo-Christian environment, in cultures that have rejected the white or the male Christ/God, in environments that are crying out for justice, what or who will be there?

My sense is that God will indeed greet those who walk where Jesus is not or has not been, or where Jesus is not welcome as presented by exclusive or patriarchal Christians. There Jesus will be, and more importantly, there Jesus will be found. We can see this, even in the particularized and unique event of Jesus, who is the precursor of things to come. Peter Berger sums up the matter this way:

> If God was in Christ, then He must be wherever redeeming power is transforming reality. This cosmic Christ, savior of this and all possible worlds. . .is everywhere, eternally. This is what was affirmed in the prologue to the Gospel of John, whose doctrine of the *logos* annexed, as it were, the entire universe of Hellenic experience: "He was in the beginning with God; all things were made through him, and without him was not anything made that was made." In other words, there are no limits to the *logos*, to Christ, in either time or space: He is present in all reality.[46]

MUTUALITY AND COMPASSION AS ARTS OF INCARNATIONAL LIVING

The whole matter of envisioning an incarnational theology would mean nothing if there were not the need and opportunity to live that theology out in practice. Again, Anglicans have viewed the Incarnation as a source for faithfulness more than as a doctrine. The practice of Incarnation, in which "God assumed humanity that we might become God,"[47] is itself a reflection of the "art of incarnational living," for in it God and humanity are related in a dynamic of mutuality and compassion. God and humankind become lovers, one of the other.

Mutuality is a dynamic of relationship, in which an economy of personhood is understood and respected. But it is also a dynamic of hospitality, that is, of welcoming the other into one's home and heart, and alternatively, receiving that welcome, that home and heart, as a gift. The dynamic of this mutuality has been of utmost importance to the renewal and development of a sense of mission in the Anglican Communion. The title of the 1963 Anglican Congress statement on mission was "Mutual Responsibility and Interdependence in the Body of Christ." It understood mutuality as primary to life together. Mutuality, as we will think of it here, is about several things: hospitality, community (*koinonia*) and the image of the Body of Christ.

In *We Are Theologians,* Fredrica Harris Thompsett describes the radical character of hospitality. It is mutuality gone scandalous. "This ministry of hospitality was more radical than toleration of difference— Jesus challenged and reversed widely accepted religious conventions."[48] Hospitality, including that of Jesus, is about acceptance of the relationship of mutuality, in which each brings to the union what they have. Thus, for Anglicans to carry with us *who we are* is not only appropriate, but necessary, if we are indeed to be in a relationship of mutuality. The scandalous character of the relationships of mutuality in which Jesus was engaged was precisely that people came as they were, and Jesus did not deny his compassion because of social and religious custom. He ate, drank, talked with, touched, and loved those in what John Dominic Crossan called "a kingdom of nuisances and nobodies."[49] Thompsett's hope, in envisioning the future of Anglican theology, is that hospitality will be a primary indicator of mission, both because it is always open to the guest, and because it always brings who we are as hosts.

> The tradition of standing for hospitality to those who are marginalized continues to encourage new life and hope for the future. Whenever Christians make room for exploring their mission capabilities, it is good to inquire, "How do we understand and how will we communicate the central traditions of our faith?"[50]

Any discussion of mutuality must acknowledge the amazing insights of John Dominic Crossan.[51] In his writings on "open commensality," he puts the matter of mutuality in the foreground of any future discussion of the art of living out the Incarnation. In a *Christian Century* article written at the time of the publication of his major study, The Historical Jesus, he defines what he means by commensality. It concerns "those decisions about what we eat, where we eat, when we eat, and, above all, with whom we eat. Taken together, these decisions form a miniature map of our social distinctions and hierarchies."[52] In this article he draws the connection between open commensality (the table where all are welcome) and healing (a wholeness large enough to hold both my diseases—my brokenness and me). The link is the notion that healing overcomes the hemorrhage of my body just as eating together overcomes the brokenness in society, by breaking down the structures of honor and shame that separate and confirm brokenness. Jesus touches the bodies and hearts of the sick. Jesus eats with the marginal.

In *Jesus: A Revolutionary Biography,* Crossan looks at another aspect of this same open commensality. Here he is concerned that we understand how radical a program it is to eat and live together, to live in mutuality:

"For those who take their very identity from the eyes of their peers, the idea of eating together and living together without distinctions, differences, discriminations, or hierarchies is close to the irrational and the absurd. And the one who advocates or does it is close to the deviant and the perverted. He has no honor. He has no shame."[53]

The Essential Jesus raises yet a third aspect of open commensality: Crossan looks at the images of Jesus available in the second century and connects them to what the earliest texts about Jesus say. He asserts that for a very long time after Jesus' death, the primary images of him were at table, eating or teaching, and healing.[54]

The open commensality of Jesus is about "binding up the wounds," eating with and healing. It is about moving into the kingdom that is present in that binding, and about the living Jesus, whom the marginal remember and the established would rather forget. The mutuality of "open commensality" is a matter of incarnational presence. The Jesus remembered is God's gracious presence in a totally available way, in which the feelings, as they say "were mutual," at least for those with no honor and no shame.

John Koenig, in *New Testament Hospitality,* builds on the notion of *koinonia* as an image of mutuality. He suggests, much more than Kettel, the Christian use of the term in its wider "secular" meaning of "a business partnership." He does so to underscore that *koinonia* is a matter of reciprocity and mutuality. It is this characteristic of New Testament hospitality that underlies his whole book—hospitality is a form of partnership in which the host and guest are intertwined in a matrix of activities. "New Testament writers conceive of partnership chiefly as cooperation in a divine project; there is a 'given' from God or Christ or the Spirit into which one enters, of which one partakes, with and for which one labors."[55]

The connection of hospitality to compassion is thus fairly direct:

> Hospitality becomes the means of reaching out to one's
> brother or sister believers, including those whom one does
> not yet know, so that new distributions of goods and services
> will come about under the aegis of God's providence . . . we
> might call hospitality the catalyst for creating and sustain-
> ing partnerships in the gospel.[56]

The "distributions of goods and services" is a direct use of the work *koinonia* in the "business partnership" sense. And the "business" of this partnership is distributive justice—that is, sharing based in compassion.

Koenig clearly sees this sort of hospitality and partnership as a partic-ular signal of God's identification with, and preference for, the marginal:

> The joy shared by Jesus and his companions reached out to
> embrace marginal people, and many of them entered it in
> the hope that it would displace the sorrows that were domi-
> nating their lives. For them, the group surrounding Jesus
> functioned as a new family where they could "receive a
> hundredfold houses and brothers and sisters and mothers
> and children and lands" (Mark 10:30).[57]

It is in the hospitality of the community that there is the first glim-mer of what it might be like to live within God's grace. For Koenig, it is the whole community, the matrix of activities within the household, that constitutes the incarnation of God's care and abundance, as the Body of Christ. It is in the concrete activities of hosting, guesting, partner-ship, and provision that compassion is realized. He closes this book with George Herbert's poem—the one known as "Love III"—as a poet-ic hint of what he understands hospitality ultimately to be about. Regarding Herbert, Koenig says, "His work stands as one of the most eloquent testimonies ever given to the power of God's hospitality."[58] In that poem, Love, God, and the Lord Jesus, are all made the host and the provision for the meal, and they make the guest the worthy guest. This is the *koinonia,* the partnership between God and Creation, made sen-sible and incarnate.

As an "art" of incarnational living, practicing hospitality is central. It is the way by which we break down the barriers that stand between us. Desmond Tutu wrote about his experience as Dean of St. Mary's Cathedral in Johannesburg:

As I have knelt in the Dean's stall at. . .High Mass with
incense, bells and everything watching a multiracial crowd
file up to the altar rails to be communicated, the one bread
and the one cup by a mixed team of clergy and lay ministers, with a multiracial choir, servers and sidemen—all this
in apartheid mad South Africa, then tears sometimes
streamed down my cheeks, tears of joy that it could be that
indeed Jesus Christ had broken down the wall of partition
and here were the first fruits of the eschatological community right here in front of my eyes.

Tutu was describing something of the crowning glory of hospitality
and mutuality. Identification with Jesus, who breaks down the walls,
and with people eating a simple meal and drinking from the same
cup—saying that it is Christ in them that lives—is what Crossan,
Koenig, and Thompsett are insisting is our vocation as people of God.

Obviously Anglicans have no special ownership of this sort of
hope. The descriptions of communities of mutuality, of open commensality, of hospitality, have always been with us. They are in many ways
the source of real and imagined communities—from the kitchen and
community of Brother Lawrence to the novel *The Clown of God* by
Morris West.

Yet it is not too much to hope that Anglicans, among the religious
bodies of this time, might take on a vocation to such hospitality. It was,
after all, in the Cathedral of St. John the Divine in New York City that
a crucifix was placed, with the crucified Christ depicted as a woman. It
was in an Anglican cathedral in South Africa in 1995 that another
image of Jesus was placed, one with the skin abrasions of the AIDS suf-
ferer. In London the Archbishop of Canterbury, at the Primates' Meeting, called English clergy to a greater knowledge of and openness to
members of other faiths, and he has modeled such a call.[59] All these
are remarkable examples of hospitality. They are also a scandal to
many Christians, even within our Anglican communities.

I have argued that Anglicans are primarily members of a fellowship, a *koinonia.* Issues of hospitality are central to fellowship, and
while we have been horribly derelict in welcoming with glad hearts and
open minds those who are our guests, or in being ourselves good guests,
at least we have been mindful that we are intimately bound up with one
another. Hooker says, "God has created nothing simply for itself; but

each thing in all things, and of everything each part in the other has such interest, that in the whole world nothing is found whereunto anything created can say, 'I need thee not.'"

In spite of grave consequences, even to his own health, the Presiding Bishop of the Episcopal Church, Edmond Browning, preached a visionary sermon at his installation in January 1986, calling the Episcopal Church to be a church in which there would be no outcasts. It is possible to take Hooker's comment and deflect it, but not so easy when we remember it is from a sermon on pride! We can take Bishop Browning's vision and begin to make exceptions, or in worldly wisdom admit to the casting out we already do, but at least the vision brings us up short.

Anglicans around the world experience in some measure the hospitality and *koinonia* and mutuality so strongly attested in our polity, in our inherence, in our collective "religion of the Incarnation." Members of our very different churches are aware of being united by bonds of mutual affection. Much of this is by way of traditions shared, by understanding of faith, as they were passed on to us and experienced. As Anglicans, we are linked by common experience in ways much stronger that our differences in particular experience would suggest. Desmond Tutu, Terry Waite, John Pobee, Fredrica Harris Thompsett, David Gituri, Barbara Harris—all may have distinctive and special experiences that form them, just as you and I do. Yet in a wonderful way, deeply related to issues of hospitality, mutuality, and *koinonia*, we are bound by common experience.

Mutuality then is a primary way for us to practice the "art of incarnational living." When we attempt to describe a vocation for Anglicans in the future, one of the descriptors must be mutuality or one of its parallels—hospitality, fellowship, and open commensality. Without that "mark," Anglican churches will be "more of the same"—closed churches, certainly closed to the marginal, and one day closed for lack of interest.

MUTUALITY AS A MARK OF ANGLICAN STYLES OF GOVERNANCE

In the Anglican Communion, mutuality is also a mark of the hospitality and openness we show to one another when we gather to do our work. It becomes a mark of governance, of the way in which the people of the church relate in carrying out the ministries they have in specific contexts, and how they collectively act as members of this order within the body of Christ.

The recent work of the Inter-Anglican Theological and Doctrinal Commission is an example of the effort to find new levels of mutuality within the communion. The Commission drew on the work of an international doctrinal consultation which met in 1992. That consultation issued a challenge to the whole communion, one that also gave direction to the Commission itself:

> The time has come for the Anglican church both locally and as a world-wide communion, to reassess its instruments of consultation and decision-making so that mutual service and commitment to Christ's mission in the world are transparently honored and addressed.[60]

The ACC placed the question of the future development of the Anglican Communion in the context of "our shared sense of vocation toward God's future."[61] It modeled and proposed certain principles of engagement:

(1) "A humane community in which there was mutual sensitivity, consideration and support, and where sharp intellectual and emotional differences as well as agreements and disagreements about theological, ethical and pastoral [issues] were possible without destroying community."[62]

(2) "Maturely interdependent Christian communities must sustain an image of the church in which there is an appreciation of the radical importance of difference, not as impediment, but as powerful catalyst. . . ."[63]

Plurality and differences were from the outset lifted up and affirmed as necessary and healthy possibilities. The affirmation of contention and struggle as part of community means that there is no recourse from honesty in engagement, and no easy interdependence. It is, however, precisely that interdependence that is at the core of "belonging together." It is nurtured by community-wide understandings of common struggle, and it is affirmed in seeking out the opportunities to do so: "At the heart of communion is the need and opportunity for interdependence."[64]

The ACC places that "need and opportunity" in the context of the Trinity, a "dynamic plurality in unity," in which there is the implication "that authority is shared within a communal life."[65] "The doctrine of the Trinity is thus understood as the single most powerful resource at the disposal of the church as it seeks to revitalize its interdependence."[66] This document then proposes that the seeming fragmentation within the communion be, if experienced in a community of mutuality, a dynamic whole.

This is clearly a statement of faith, grounding the struggles toward ongoing interdependence on the model of a doctrine that itself is understood only partially. It is this statement that in turn gives the ACC a heart to suggest that our interdependence in the Anglican Communion is neither fully understood nor lived, and that the task of moving toward a "fuller interdependence" is the future of the communion itself. In that task the ACC particularly points to issues of structure on national and international levels. It does so because it sees these bodies exercising two functions central to interdependence:

> First and most important, is the exchange of information and insight in which conversation and argument can continue as long as necessary without institutionalizing disagreement either geographically or by schism. Second, it is a process which allows the communion to discern God's will, reach a common mind and speak authoritatively at appropriate points in the process of reception.[67]

At the close of the document an important note on sources of authority is made, particularly as it relates to the discussion here on mutuality, *koinonia* and hospitality. The ACC affirmed that Anglicans appeal to "the authority dispersed in the bonds of interdependence."[68]After acknowledging diocesan and provincial authority, it then says,

> There are three other sources of authority which overlap but are not coterminous: the authority of church leaders by election or appointment to office, the authority inherent in professional competence and, not least, the authority of men and women who by prayer, loving relationships and reflection on daily experience have grown wise in holy living and exercise a profoundly prophetic role in the life of the church.[69]

This is a remarkably Anglican document, filled with concerns for a widening mutuality in the church. It is clear example of how issues of governance continue to be intertwined with the insights of experience within the communion.

COMPASSION AS A MARK OF ANGLICAN STYLES OF ENGAGEMENT

Mutuality is most often thought of as a dynamic between friends, between members of the same body. It has been mostly thought of as a way of viewing *koinonia.* For this reason I have earlier suggested that the Greek *koinonia* be translated "community of mutuality." *Koinonia* is often used to describe the Anglican Communion, and certainly the meetings of its bishops and other church leadership. And of course, the "Mutual" in "Mutual Responsibility and Interdependence" is about fellowship/*koinonia.* But what about the hospitality to strangers and the openness that breaks down barriers? Surely that is not a matter *within* the fellowship?

Mutuality only describes one element of the "art of incarnational living." The other great element is found in *compassion.* Unlike the words related to the household of the faith—mutuality, unity in the body, hospitality, fellowship—compassion is mutuality related to "those far off as well as those who are near." Jesus had compassion on the multitudes (Matt. 9:36) and on two blind men (Matt. 18:21); we would say, "His heart went out to them." The Greek places the feeling more in the gut. But in both, instances, compassion is shown by a pull toward others. The others, as in the crowd or the blind men, may not be members of *koinonia* at all. Yet the pull toward them is an act of incarnational living.[70] Jesus has compassion, and as partners in the Incarnation so must we. But in what does this compassion consist?

Those marginalized by the principalities and powers, and who still talk to us, talk of God's compassion and the presence of that compassion in Jesus Christ. The link between mercy and justice, on the one hand, and the pull of the heart and the gut, on the other, is established in the minds of the oppressed. It remains for those of us who do not easily understand the Incarnation of compassion to make, as much as in us lies, the same preference that God and Jesus Christ make for the poor.

Gregory Baum, in *Compassion and Solidarity,* a transcript of five radio talks he gave on the Canadian Broadcasting Company network, tries to describe the Canadian, and to some extent North American, consequences of the remarkable "new movement in the Christian churches that creates a startling link between religious faith and concern for others. What has taken place in the Christian religion is an outburst of compassion."[71] Baum tells a mostly Roman Catholic story, but one that has its parallels in other major North American churches and says much to our exploration here. The "outburst of compassion" of which he speaks began following the Second World War. For Protestants, a beginning signal was the development of the World Council of Churches in 1948. For Roman Catholics, it was the work that led to and the statements that issued from the Second Vatican Council.[72] The first efforts to really respond to others in a "gut" way grew from two new activities of churches: ecumenical and inter-religious solidarity in the face of the Holocaust and the worldwide horrors of the war, and conversation among churches and between churches and peoples of other faiths that grew in strength to a place of solidarity and greater acceptance of religious pluralism. In turn, this led to greater individual and collective church efforts to address the horrors that the war had so clearly shown, but which were now seen to continue in many forms.

It is this solidarity that later becomes the basis of liberation theology, and it is here that the connection between Incarnation at the one pole, and compassion at the other, is seen. "This process [liberation], when looked upon with the eyes of faith, reveals itself as part of a wider and deeper transformation, grounded in God's redeeming presence, affecting all aspects of human life, spiritual and material."[73] God's redeeming presence is an *incarnational* notion, and the "transformation. . .affecting all aspects of human life" is the compassion of God, shown in what liberation theology came to call "God's preferential option for the poor."[74]

Baum identifies the theological underpinnings of the solidarity movement with God's immanence in the world. "God is the matrix out of which we move forward, the vector that directs our lives, and the horizon toward which we are called. . . .God is graciously present in human history, . . .enlightening and empowering people to build a more human society"[75]

Lest solidarity be considered a simple thing, Baum introduces the notion that what solidarity and Incarnation (immanence) first means for the affluent is known negatively: God graciously present in human history is not God as the church has known God. He describes this in two experiences, "the dread of ideological distortion" and "the breakdown of trust."[76]

The first is the problem that the God known to the affluent is a false god. And this fact leads the follower in a negative path that can end in despair. It is necessary, he contends, to face into that despair and anguish and to move on from there. He quotes Johann Baptist Metz, who lived this negative way in relation to the Holocaust. His theological principle for moving beyond the anguish of the negative way is this: "You cannot do theology with your back turned to Auschwitz."[77]

The second experience, the breakdown of trust, leads to the question, Even if one may do theology after Auschwitz, can one pray? "Jews and Christians who still think of themselves as religious must continue to ask the question whether it is possible to pray after Auschwitz. They experience not a theoretical but an existential doubt. They try to pray but find it impossible. They listen but there is no voice and no melody. Deep down they, too, no longer trust God."[78]

These are two experiences of the negative way Baum considers the paradox of our time: To believe that God is a God of compassion is to identify God not with our "comfortable words," but with God's comfort, which is for the poor. And that means that, as affluent people, we cannot trust our words and, if we know the enormity of the pain of the world, we cannot trust God. The way out of the paradox is to pass through the "via negativa" to the "via eminentae, the way of expanded meaning."[79] It is here that Baum's incarnational theology is finally realized. The expanded meaning is in God's immanence in the world, in God's life beyond the limits of the religious community. It is in this context, I believe, that the other side of the notion of "God's preferential option for the poor" is found. If God has a preferential option for the poor, when the poor enter the partnership of host-guest, it will be in the face of the poor that we meet God. That is, the church, which has waited for the return of the Christ, meets the Christ in the poor.

With mutuality, compassion is a primary mark of the incarnational community when it heals and seeks justice. It is known primarily in reconciliation, in the move to restore to unity. A wide variety of Anglican theologians have seen the Incarnation, particularly as it bridges the gap between God and humanity (or the cosmos), as the source of compassionate living.[80] That compassion is widely evidenced in the church as it goes about reaching out to those who are not now, nor likely ever to be, members of this particular religious community. It is also known in the occasions where members of the church have reached across the barriers, as did Jesus, drawing out, as well as drawing in.

It must also be said, unfortunately, that just as Anglican churches have never been able to decide to become "peace churches," but rather have tried to be "peace-making churches," so it is also true that Anglican churches have had a good deal of difficulty in being as compassionate as the Jesus for whom we witness. We are too often willing to care for rather than be compassionate with others.

We do see compassion sometimes in members of our relatively small fellowship who have crossed the lines of closed commensalities and eaten, drunk, talked, laughed, healed, and died with and for others. Some few are known, but most are unknown. It seems to me one way in which we exhibit the mark of compassion is by supporting one another in acts of courage. *Courageous Incarnation* is an appropriate title for a book on incarnational living, for it points in two directions— toward having the courage to be the body of Christ, and the courage to take on its tasks.[81]

Earlier I listed fellowship as one of the traditional marks of Anglican church life and of the Anglican Communion. To it—because of the continued strength of Anglican witness to the Incarnation—I now add mutuality and compassion. Given the framework which these marks provide, and with a courage that I hope echoes that known in the Incarnation, I want to close with specific vocational recommendations for the Anglican churches and the Anglican Communion. While much of what I have written has seemed preparatory to this specific end, I hope the process itself has led the reader to think too of our vocational future as a fellowship within Christ's church.

ENDNOTES

1. Cox, *Many Mansions*, 8.

2. In my use of the word hospitable I am following the practice of Thompsett, *Courageous Incarnation in Intimacy, Work, Childhood and Aging*, 4; idem, *We Are Theologians*, 128ff.

3. Stendahl, "From God's Perspective We Are All Minorities," 6.

4. Russell, *Church in the Round*, 130.

5. Stendhal, ibid., 2.

6. Ibid., 4–5.

7. Ibid., 3.

8. Cox, ibid.

9. Ibid., 73.

10. Cox, ibid., 2.

11. Berger, *A Far Glory*, 145–46.

12. Ibid., 146–47.

13. Cone, *God of the Oppressed*, 73.

14. Ibid., 76–77.

15. Ibid., 110–11.

16. In *A Black Theology of Liberation*, 2nd ed. (1986), Cone makes greater use of Bonhoeffer, but primarily in reference to moral action against oppression.

17. Cone, *God of the Oppressed*, 135.

18. Bonhoeffer, *Christ the Center*, 110–18.

19. Cone, ibid., 137.

20. Idem, *A Black Theology of Liberation*, 117.

21. Heyward, *Speaking of Christ*, 23–25.

22. Ibid., 24.

23. Ibid., 19.

24. Ibid., 26n.

25. Michael Goulder, "Jesus, the Man of Universal Destiny," in Hick, ed. *The Myth of God Incarnate*, 62.

26. Heyward, *Speaking of Christ*, 21.

27. Thompsett, *Courageous Incarnation*, 12.

28. Ibid., 4.

29. Ibid., 14.

30. Heyward, *Speaking of Christ*, 21.

31. Thompsett, ibid., 24.

32. Tutu, *Hope and Suffering*, 125.

33. Tutu, "The Theologian and the Gospel of Freedom," in Eaton: *The Trial of Faith: Theology and the Church Today*, 63–64.

34. Idem, *Hope and Suffering*, ibid.

35. Ibid., 34.

36. Song, *The Compassionate God*, 160.

37. Ibid., 16.

38. Ibid.

39. Ibid., 17.

40. Ibid., 4.

41. Ibid., 11.

42. Ibid., 12.

43. Song, 181.

44. Thompsett, ibid., 19; citing Sallie McFague, *Models of God* (Philadelphia: Fortress Press, 1987), 136.

45. Thompsett, ibid.

46. Berger, *A Far Glory*, 166.

47. Irenaeus, *The Scandal of the Incarnation*, 93.

48. Thompsett, *We Are Theologians*, 129.

49. Crossan, *Jesus: A Revolutionary Biography*, title of chap. 3.

50. Thompsett, ibid., 132.

51. I am aware that Crossan receives a great deal of criticism; but in terms of the challenge of his imagery, he has placed the specifics of Jesus' actions back on the table for discussion in ways that are both effective and powerful.

52. Crossan, "The Life of a Mediterranean Jewish Peasant," *The Christian Century*, Vol. 108, No. 37, 1195.

53. Idem, *Jesus: A Revolutionary Biography*, 70.

54. Idem, *The Essential Jesus*, 11–13, 18.

55. Ibid., 8.

56. Ibid., 10.

57. Ibid., 29.

58. Ibid., 146.

59. Press release: Episcopal News Service, March 10, 1995.

60. ACC, Inter-Anglican Theological and Doctrinal Commission: *Belonging Together*, 24.

61. Ibid., 3.

62. Ibid., 4.

63. Ibid., 5.

64. Ibid., 4.

65. Ibid., 15.

66. Ibid.

67. Ibid., 25.

68. Ibid., 26.

69. Ibid.

70. It is interesting to note that Jesus has compassion of the gut-wrenching sort, just as you and I have (the Greek for "compassion" meaning "to have the bowels yearn"). But God is compassionate as an aspect of mercy.

71. Baum, *Compassion and Solidarity*, 11.

72. Ibid., 12–13.

73. Ibid., 24.

74. Ibid., 28.

75. Ibid., 72–73.

76. Ibid., 77.

77. Ibid., 79.

78. Ibid., 82.

79. Ibid., 86.

80. Matthew Fox, whose contributions to the understanding of the relation between cosmos and compassion are quite remarkable, has become an Anglican. See his *A Spirituality Named Compassion*, 2nd ed

81. Thompsett, *Courageous Incarnation*.

CHAPTER 5

A VOCATIONAL MANIFESTO
FOR THE ANGLICAN
COMMUNION

At the beginning of this century Frank Westcott wrote a book with
a wonderfully long title: *Catholic Principles, as Illustrated in the
Doctrine, History and Organization of the American Catholic Church in
the United States, commonly called the Protestant Episcopal Church.* In
this he spoke glowingly of the future growth of Anglicanism. In a
moment of triumphalist bliss he wrote that if trends continued, the
Archbishop of Canterbury would soon replace the Bishop of Rome as
the leader of the largest communion in Christendom.[1] Chief among his
cited reasons were the numbers of Roman Catholic clergy joining the
Episcopal Church as a reformed Catholic body. At the end of this century, in much less triumphal, but equally glowing terms, Roger White
and Richard Kew believe that, "the Episcopal Church (through its
social ministries, intellectual life and spirituality) will continue to
attract people who will find their faith enriched in our Communion."[2]
They believe "clarity of Anglican identity will be an important factor in
bringing in outsiders to our tradition."[3] They, too, find comfort and
tantalizing possibilities in the movement of Roman Catholic and conservative Protestant clergy and congregations into the Episcopal
Church. The beginning and the end of the century are thus marked by

popular texts that claim that Anglicans will attract people looking for what it has to offer. Both are clear that it will happen only if being Anglican or Episcopalian is a viable alternative for those who are coming from more conservative theological backgrounds. White and Kew quote John H. Rogers, who noted that these conservatives will

> continue to come if we do not move in a dramatically liberal direction. As I read their mood, they wish to add the liturgical, sacramental, and historical dimensions without violating their evangelical convictions. A church that has lurched into an obviously liberal posture would not, I think, attract them.[4]

FACING INTO THE POST-MODERN WORLD

Religious practice within Anglican communities is indeed attractive to many. I am quite convinced that we have much to offer the world, particularly as Kew and White have suggested, in a faith grounded liturgically, sacramentally, and historically. However, when I consider vocational directions for Anglican churches or the Anglican Communion, it is not its possible growth in numbers that excites me. Indeed, if that growth were by virtue of acquiring or maintaining conservative theological convictions, I am not at all sure what we would have gained. I am not sure we would even gain numbers. What most excites me about the vocational directions possible for the Anglican Communion is that *if we keep the faith,* we can be reasonably useful carriers of the good news of Jesus Christ into an increasingly pluralistic, post-modern world. Anglicans are on the whole suited to this task by our theological grounding, our method, and our practice. More, our experience has made us willing to live provisionally. We await the day when the wounds will be healed, and when God's restorative call to unity will be met by our willingness to become what God wills, rather than what we will. Along the way, we may for a time attract people to the various Anglican churches. But we know in faith what the bishops in Chicago in 1886 were willing to proclaim,

> that in all things of human ordering or human choice, relating to modes of worship and discipline, or to traditional customs, this Church is ready in the spirit of love and humility

> to forego all preferences of her own, (and) that this Church
> does not seek to absorb other Communions, but rather, co-
> operating with them on the basis of a common Faith and
> Order, to discountenance schism, to heal the wounds of the
> Body of Christ, and to promote the charity which is the chief
> of Christian graces and the visible manifestation of Christ to
> the world.[5]

The willingness to live out that faith, forgoing all preferences and promoting charity, will sometimes lead others to join us. It will also lead almost *inevitably* to the emergence in all parts of the Anglican Communion of *post-Anglican Christian bodies* that will claim us as their forbears.

Short-term interest in Anglican church growth is not particularly helpful when thinking of vocational recommendations for the communion, because it is essentially a trap. It leads us to the temptation to think of size as a vocation and strategies for growth as recommendations. We would then promote various reunion efforts for the wrong reasons, namely the propagation of Anglicanism *per se*. It would perhaps lead to growth in the short run, but no real expansion. I am *not* suggesting that we should not try to grow by attracting people, or by joining together like-minded Christian communities. Indeed, we should make every effort to do so. But our reason should not be related to comparisons in size with, say, the Methodists or Lutherans or Roman Catholics. Rather, we should be interested in growth because we are more interested in finding Jesus Christ in community than in being Anglican. And I am not suggesting that we should dismiss the Anglican experience. Far from it! Our communities have much to offer the emerging forms of Christian life. God willing and our faithfulness enabling, we will be the door through which many will walk on their way to life in Christ; but we must guard against too strong a commitment to our door as *the* door.

The English concern for Anglican identity seems primarily to treat identity as a matter of consistency. Some English thinkers raise the question, "Do Anglicans stand together on matters of doctrine and practice?" What is sought is an identity that sets Anglicans apart from other Christian groups. In the United States the matter seems more related to the question, "What do Anglicans stand for (and parenthetically, what do Anglicans stand against)?" The question is not one of consistency, but of orthodoxy. Kew and White see the trends moving away from "theological speculation" and toward a "dynamic orthodoxy."[6] But the concerns on both sides of the ocean are oddly similar, in that both English and U.S. Anglicans draw back from a trust in their ability to live faithfully on the basis of the experience in community. Both English and U.S. efforts seem guided not so much by the desire to be correct as by the desire to have a market share based on product recognition. The call for consistency and orthodoxy is driven by the supposition that doctrine sells well, while process in community does not.

I have suggested earlier that we might think of ourselves as members of a religious community or order, with a rule and a way of life, rather than as a church with peculiar doctrines and a particular structure. As I reflect on the difference between these two models, I am more and more convinced of the vocational effectiveness of the first and the vocationally debilitating character of the second. If we are an order, we can attend to those things that keep us together without insisting that these things are essential to the faith and available only through us. In other words, our provisionality will work to our benefit and charity, rather than to our detriment.

In recommending directions for the Anglican Communion and Anglican churches for the next period of time, I am very aware of not wanting to repeat the efforts of Westcott or those of Kew and White. As I suggested in the beginning of this work, this is neither a set of predictive remarks nor a description of trends. Rather, my recommendations represent a vision for the future of the communion. I believe that working for something like this vision is valuable and faithful, because I believe these recommendations honor our experience. More importantly, the vision honors our commitment to Jesus Christ, whose incarnational presence, mutuality, and compassion ground our faith.

This vision builds on the elements of religious community that are almost always part of our concern when Anglicans come together to discuss the present life of the communion and its future. I will want to look briefly at elements of a vision that build on incarnational faith, Anglican method, the marks of community, and the experience of prayer and life together.

Trusting the experience of Christian community is possible only when it is realized that *all such communities are incarnational.* That is, all Christian communities are to one extent or another the incarnation of God's will to unity, contextualized by location and history. The location, however, makes all such communities limited in their ability to reflect the fullness of God's will to unity. The search for identity has led some Anglicans to want to make Anglicanism a universal ideology, so that Anglican churches can be seen to share common doctrine identified with orthodoxy or the truth. But the fact is that Anglicans exist in contextually determined communities. We must come to trust that God is using our struggles with, as well as our agreement on, doctrine and practice to a good end.

LIVING PROVISIONALLY

The willingness to live out the particularity of incarnation leads to a first observation: The gospel, not the church, is the first priority in our vocation.[7] On a practical level Anglican churches must hold themselves and the communion accountable to the spiritual and prophetic assertion of the gospel of Jesus Christ in the world. It must at the same time acknowledge the widely varied contexts in which that accountability must be expressed. We will not be "of one mind," nor will there be unanimity on spiritual and moral practice. Our unity will be tried, and we may in fact be broken, by our differences. The guiding factor in our vocation will not, however, be in our unity *as Anglicans,* but rather in our unity as followers of Jesus Christ. We must be clear that our vocation is not to be *the* church having *the* truth, but rather a fellowship accountable to the gospel and expressing that accountability in our fellowship as we break bread and say the prayers.

Here is an example of my concerns in this area: I have an African-made crucifix on my wall on which the corpus is clearly that of a black man. The gospel calls me to wrestle with Jesus' suffering and its meaning, and the black African Christ on my wall puts that suffering in a special location vis-à-vis my life as a white American. It speaks to me in a central way of the gospel. The crucifix was given to me by a friend from the (Anglican) Church in the Province of Kenya. We are both

Anglicans, but we are quite different from one another. He and his church have viewed polygamy quite differently from my church. My church has viewed divorce differently than has his. We have widely different liturgical practice. We have considerable difference in our understanding of the role of women in the church. Our understanding of the value and character of missionary work, denominations, and even charitable work are quite different. What then draws us together? The gospel, understood as well as we are able in our contexts, and our willingness to look there rather than only at our differences for the possibility of relationship. We are drawn together because we wish to be drawn together in the Body of Christ.

Anglicans are a provisional people and should remain so. The differences among the churches of the communion on matters of community morality are extensive. These are popularly understood to be differences of opinion concerning the ordering of persons in the ministry of the sacraments who were previously considered by class or caste as unsuitable (women, people of color, homosexuals, the physically handicapped, etc.), or about the admission generally of such persons into sacramental relationship with the church (baptism of polygamists, remarriage of divorced persons, etc.), or about the holding of correct belief or doctrine (the authority of scripture and the creeds). We can, however, hold positions different from one another, but understand them to be *provisional*, rather than absolute. Underlying all these issues is the ongoing struggle to live together with a rather broad range of provisionally held convictions. If we fail in this effort to gather around the table with all that provisionality implies, we will cease to be Anglican.

We Anglicans do and will have strong opinions, and make claims to conscience that may draw us out of the Anglican community and indeed out of Christendom. Churches in the Anglican Communion are and will be in different places (locations) regarding social and ecclesial concerns. If we break communion over them, we will essentially be saying that we can no longer stand provisionality. That, of course, may be exactly what some need to do, but I think it will be done with deep sadness.

An example of the "provisionality of our provisionality" can be found in the presentation of Desmond Tutu to the Eloff Commission in 1982. Regarding apartheid, he said,

> I will demonstrate that apartheid, separate development or whatever it is called is evil, totally and without remainder, that it is unchristian and unbiblical. . . .If anybody were to show me that apartheid is biblical or Christian, I have said before and I reiterate now, that I would burn my Bible and cease to be a Christian. I will want to show that the Christian Bible and the Gospel of Jesus Christ our Lord is subversive of all injustice and evil, oppression and exploitation. . . .

Clearly there are limits to what Christians can tolerate, and it is within the purview of Anglicans to describe those limits, even if they lead to the rejection of Christianity itself. We need to have the clarity that Tutu had. But we also need his willingness to make provisional even Scripture or his affiliation as a Christian when the cause of justice is at stake. At the same time, I believe that his willingness to live in faith *provisionally* rests in the profound confidence that the Bible and the gospel are in fact the great witness to the presence of a just God in the creation.

In the past few years there have been particular examples of events in the Anglican Communion that have presented great difficulties for the communion, but which have not led to formal breaks in the fellowship of the churches. In particular the ordination of women to the priesthood has severely stretched our fellowship. There have been de facto breaks, as for example when those supporting the universal validity of orders have refused to celebrate or participate in the celebration of the eucharist where women were deliberately excluded from priestly roles, or where bishops in various parts of the communion have refused to accept women priests in their dioceses. These have been deeply disturbing breaks in fellowship, but the primates have resolutely refused to break communion over issues surrounding the ordination of women, preferring a provisional and partial set of solutions. Those groups of Anglicans who have left the Episcopal Church to establish so-called "continuing" Anglican churches have not been able to live with that provisionality.[8]

Provisionality is not an easy vocational stance. It must be clearly distinguished from "blowing neither hot nor cold." As I have tried to indicate, I believe provisionality is a deeply understood and experienced methodological stance within Anglican thought. Difficult to live with, it would be even more difficult to live without. At least it acknowledges in practice what we know to be true: "We know only in part, and we prophesy only in part; but when the complete comes, the partial will come to an end" (1 Cor. 13: 9–10).

Look again at the marks of Anglican life, discussed earlier as (1) fellowship, (2) in the one, holy, catholic, and apostolic church, (3) in communion with the See of Canterbury, (4) having historic Faith and Order, as (5) described in the Book of Common Prayer. These marks give us another way to open out to a vocation for the Anglican Communion in the future. Pictured as a fellowship, rather than a church (*koinonia* rather than *ekklesia*) the Anglican Communion and Anglican churches are the signs of people living in an ordered way, as a religious community. If this is our fellowship, one would expect us to identify ourselves by how we pray, eat, think and speak, rather than identify ourselves by the beliefs of our specific church. And, in fact, that is precisely what has happened in our experience.

We have been remarkably consistent in our unwillingness to claim a special knowledge of correct Christian belief or doctrine. When Anglican theologians have done their work they have mostly wrestled with what they understand to be the faith received and lived out in the prayers and the breaking of bread and in actions in the world, without assuming a centrality to Anglican forms or understandings. We have said, and continue to say, that what we do is, in so far as possible, decent and in order. Yet the cautionary note of the Preface to the 1549 Book of Common Prayer continues to be operative, "There was never any thing by the wit of man so well devised, or so surely established, which (in continuance of time) hath not been corrupted. . . ."[9] That mark of provisionality is a vocation in itself.

If we were other than a fellowship, we would become even more entangled in the sinfulness of the separation within Christendom. If we really believe we are the primary example, or the only example, of orthodoxy, then we should say so and call all people to join us in the true faith. But of course we do not. So we cannot issue a call for all to join us as the standard bearers of the truth. Rather, we can invite persons into our fellowship, and perhaps more radically, open ourselves out to people and communities, in ways that reflect the "open commensality" and hospitality that Crossan and others find in Jesus' mission.

We cannot say that we have been at all good at this in the past, but on the whole we have been reticent to claim more for our way of being Christian than we ought. Perhaps the reformation emphasis on our limitations, understood in the light of the doctrine of justification by faith alone and echoed in our confessions of sin, has born fruit. People in the Anglican fellowship understand, at least sometimes, that the limitations of the carriers of the gospel are in the carriers and not the gospel they carry.

The mark of the "One, Holy, Catholic, and Apostolic Church" is in a way the mirror of the mark of fellowship, for it is the description of what it is that we do claim is the *ekklesia*. If we are not the church, what is? There is no entity existing in Christendom that is this church—there is no "one" church; there is no especially singled out "holy" church; there is no "apostolic" church. I would suggest that such an entity has never existed, and that even from its inception, division, sinfulness, and "new and strange" practices appeared in the church. In that sense, the mark of the "One, Holy, Catholic, and Apostolic Church" is a mark of our future, not of our past. It is the mark that sets our goal, rather than the place we came from. That is why the branch diagram of the history of Christian church development is so deceptive. Only two historical places hold the unity we speak of in this mark—the literal incarnation of God in Jesus Christ, and the Body of Christ that constitutes the church at the end of the age. For the time being, the mark is known only in the longed-for completion of things.

THE MATRIX MODEL FOR COMMUNION

The way in which unity has been effected in the Anglican Communion is perhaps one of our greatest gifts to the whole church. We are not "tidy," but the ways in which we have "knit together" this particular elect are an important study in what has been called conciliar Christianity. The commitment to mutuality is very strong in the communion, and is expressed on many levels. There are several focal points in this knitting that will need some work in the next period: How do we describe the issue of communion in a way that changes the focus from "communion with the See of Canterbury" to "a matrix of communion"?

How are those deliberations—the Lambeth Conference, the Anglican Consultative Council, the Primates' Meetings, etc., and the committees of the ACC—to be understood? What happens when Anglican jurisdictions become post-Anglican (the Church in China or in South India)? These questions are central to the issue of mutuality, and finally to what we hold at the core of the phrase "in communion with the See of Canterbury."

As it stands now, most member churches of the Anglican Communion are in *de facto* communion with Canterbury, although the basis of that communion has been historically determined by the succession of bishops rather than by concordat or church agreement. If there is anywhere a statement of intent to continue the religious tradition of the Church of England, it is most often found in the Prayer Books of the communion that acknowledge their indebtedness to the English book of 1662 and maintain doctrinal agreement with that book. There are however some churches, such as those of Spain and Portugal, the Philippine Independent Church, and the Old Catholic bodies, that are related to Canterbury or other provincial bodies by deliberate and overt action—by concordat or agreement. This process goes on, witness the Provo agreement between the Church of England and the Lutheran bodies in Europe and England, and the Concordat being considered between the Episcopal and Lutheran bodies in the United States. And of course, there are the Churches of South and North India and Pakistan, whose communion with the Anglican Communion was supported by the Lambeth Conference approval of the union schemes. All of this is pointing to a pattern that will only become more complex in the years ahead. The notion that the Anglican Communion consists of those churches simply in communion with the See of Canterbury is not now very useful. In the future it will not hold. The lines of communion and communication will need to move to being a matrix rather than single connections between the provinces and Canterbury.

An important example of this need for matrix definition of our connections is seen in the efforts between the Church of England and the English Methodists to unite. What happens if they are able to unite, while at the same time Methodists and Anglicans elsewhere are not able to do so? The Archbishop of Canterbury might invite a much wider range of church representatives to his or her table than is now represented by "churches in communion with the See of Canterbury." (The Archbishop can of course do this now.) Some of those would be in communion with their counterparts in other countries where those were not in communion with the Anglican communities. The anomalies could become quite extensive.

On the whole, Anglicans seem willing to risk a time of considerable confusion in order to continue with reunion schemes. In doing so, however, we must work at being clear about just what we mean when we talk of being in communion, if only so that we do not offend or reject precisely those whose brothers and sisters we are. My sense is that we need to move beyond the rather simple, one-way test of communion status. It will become less important to ask whom the Archbishop of Canterbury invites to Lambeth and more interesting to ask how the bishops will collectively open themselves to others. Similarly, it will be less important that we see the Archbishop of Canterbury as a spiritual head of the communion, and more interesting to see the web of ongoing relationships among primates, bishops, and dioceses as central.

THE ROLE OF THE ARCHBISHOP OF CANTERBURY

In the not too distant future the Anglican Communion will begin to disburse the spiritual authority that the more ecclesial-minded have assigned to the Archbishop of Canterbury. That action will echo the dispersal of authority seen in Anglican practice elsewhere. Provinces have always set their own directions, while at the same time being committed by bonds of mutuality to attend to one another's opinions and concerns. But the history of the controversy concerning the ordination of women shows clearly that mutuality is well served in the context of disbursed authority in ways that it is not when there is only a single source of authority.[10]

At some point the definition of the Anglican Communion will not rely on the direct connection with the See of Canterbury. That in turn will mean that some of what connects us will cease to be determined by things English. The Lambeth Conference may in the future meet outside England, with someone else in the chair. Given our propensity to do things with tradition and honor, Canterbury will still continue to have a seat of honor, but less often the central seat.

I must admit a real concern about the reduction of the Archbishop of Canterbury's power of invitation without new schemes put in place to make decisions concerning invitation into the Anglican Communion. Churches in internal leadership crisis are challenged and helped by knowing that Canterbury has a stake in overcoming organizational schism. Canterbury either directly or through the Anglican Consultative Council has been directly beneficial to maintaining unity in the midst of the stresses caused by the various issues of the time.[11] No doubt there will be more to come. However, mutuality and disbursed authority will make it more attractive to think in terms of a communion matrix rather than a unidirectional link with Canterbury.

All of this assumes, of course, a vocational direction somewhat different from that envisioned by those who hope for a stronger center for an international Anglican Communion, or who wish for doctrinal clarity in a way that can be enforced for churches belonging to the communion. The vision of a worldwide Anglican Communion that *stands for something uniquely Anglican* is very attractive to some. The idea of an international church is expressed symbolically in the call for some form of an Anglican Patriarchate, much like that of Rome or Constantinople. The Archbishop of Canterbury is often treated like that, and I share the pride in knowing that the Anglican fellowship is regarded so highly by world churches. I am also delighted to see the Archbishop considered a spiritual leader on the world level. I am concerned when the expectation begins to be voiced that we need greater unity of doctrine so that the Archbishop can come to the table with a distinctively Anglican perspective in hand both to present outwardly in the ecumenical sphere, and to judge within the communion.

THE ROLE OF THE PRAYER BOOK

Out of the concerns for mutuality, disbursed authority, and matrix-defined communion, another element of the vocation to a common life requires attention, that of the role of the Book of Common Prayer. Stephen Sykes echoes the concern many have about the Book of

Common Prayer as the touchstone of Anglican theology and doctrine. He said,

> There is no discernible agreement that the undeniably English (and Scottish) origins of the worldwide communion have bestowed on it lasting spiritual benefits. In particular those Prayer Books (the English and the Scottish) which previously provided much of the family ethos to the whole Church are now undergoing extensive revision on a purely local basis, each autonomous Province holding itself to be competent to revise its liturgy without reference to any other. The result is inevitably an apparently ever-increasing pluralism, without discernible restraint or boundaries.

Certainly Anglicans are no longer bound by a single prayer book. It is even less evident that we are committed to books that carry the same doctrinal or theological accents of the "standard" book of 1662. But the idea that there are no "discernible restraint or boundaries" is overstated.

Most provinces have put liturgical reform in the hands of those most qualified, and one of the peculiar characteristics of those interested in liturgy is their high regard for history on the one hand, and context on the other. In most parts of the communion the received tradition plays a large part in the theological formation of the very people who will recommend any changes. Liturgical revision seems restrained and bound to a considerable extent by the methods we use, by methods grounded in scripture, tradition, and reason.

The elements of Anglican method, and the principles that lay behind the initial development of the Book of Common Prayer and the style of "unity by inclusion," provide Anglicans with a reasonable way forward in liturgical revision. No doubt the changes will lead away from the Book of Common Prayer of 1662, but they will mostly do so responsibly, moving us toward and beyond "where we might have traveled on our own."

It will not be possible to refer in the future to a specific Prayer Book and claim that as our basis for theology and doctrine. It is somewhat questionable that we ever could, for from the beginning, new books, particularly the Scottish and American books, drew on materials that subtly changed the received English book and its sacramental theology. But it will be possible, and indeed it will be all the more necessary, to adopt liturgical forms, texts and practice that are taken from the worship life of other churches.

Anglican Prayer Books have even migrated from the use of the title, "The Book of Common Prayer." In some places the books in common use are "Alternative Services" to the Book of Common Prayer. In Australia the book in use is called "An Australian Prayer Book." In the Church of the Province of South Africa it is not "The Book of Common Prayer," but "A Book of Common Prayer," saving the title "The Book of Common Prayer" as reference to the English book of 1662. Yet the assumption of the Book(s) of Common Prayer, by whatever name, has been *religious community* in which both the sacramental and disciplined prayer life are essential. The new books carry on that idea whatever their name, in part by the acknowledgment that their origins are to be found in the "standard" English Book and the round of liturgical actions it proposes.

One of the most serious difficulties faced by the various books is the growing Anglican and ecumenical emphasis on the eucharist as the standard for prayer when the community gathers. For example, in many parts of the Episcopal Church, the common use of morning or evening prayer has all but disappeared. The laudable reaffirmation of the eucharist as the principal service on Sundays has not been accompanied by a renewal of daily morning and evening prayer in public or private contexts. At some point in the future a simple Sunday eucharist pamphlet or book may replace the Book of Common Prayer as the tool needed for the whole of the common worship experience of most Episcopalians. When that happens, American Anglicans will have lost a great inheritance and a liturgical context for the round of daily prayer and scripture reading. They will also lose great reading material when looking for something to do during a long and boring sermon. I knew all about the prayers for the sick, the Thirty-Nine Articles and the Psalter long before personal need or seminary drove me to them!

The community at prayer—in common prayer—has been the assumed basis for the spirituality of Anglicanism. In a way Anglican spiritual practice has also assumed that people live close to places of common worship and with work patterns determined by the sun's rise and set. Does Anglican daily prayer still assume the village and the village church? One hopes not, but it does assume the gathering of community. We often overlook the fact that what is distinctly and historically Anglican about our worship assumes that community is possible and readily at hand. Those of us interested in keeping the Book of Common Prayer ought to be much more concerned with the formation of community in our particularly fragmented world than we are with being either doctrinally pure or organizationally specific, or for that matter committed to the continuation of the use of the Book of Common Prayer itself.

THE PROBLEMS OF FRAGMENTATION

There are good reasons to suggest that addressing the fragmentation of community be a primary task of the church at the end of the age of modernity. Larry Rasmussen, in *Moral Fragments and Moral Community*, begins his work with a conclusion: "Our society [the United States] currently lives from moral fragments and community fragments only, and both are being destroyed faster than they are being replenished. This bodes trouble. . . ."[12] His question is, "Given the claims of Christian faith, and given the requirements of moral formation in a society like ours, indeed a world like ours, what is the shape proper to the church? What are its contributions as a community of moral conviction?"[13]

Rasmussen quickly goes on to say that of course it is not only moral conviction, but *which* moral conviction, that is the issue. Somehow the effort to live in community must be accompanied by means of discernment and limitations on hubris. One would hope that part of the cohesiveness of a commendable "community of moral conviction" would be found in its forms common prayer and sacraments. For prayer and sacrament to serve the discernment function in the community, they would have to transcend the specifics of the community (its location) and at the same time be relevant to it. The notion of a common prayer for a whole people does just that—it brings into each local community matters relevant to its life and yet not totally dependent on it.

In a world of increasing fragmentation, the particular spirituality and piety that undergirds the Prayer Book offices and sacraments assumes and encourages community. The culturally rich and diverse elements that make up the prayers and practices of these books themselves are part of the guarantee that the books are not mere echoes of the morals of a specific society or culture. The Prayer Books of the Anglican churches mostly refer to local gatherings of a worldwide faithful community in their intercessions. The local community (the *koinonia*) comes together as the assembly of God's people—the church (the *ekkesia*), the fellowship is itself a part of the Body of Christ. Rasmussen sees the local community of mutuality committed to following "the Way." Such communities identify themselves as "people of the Way"[14] who, in their gatherings can do much to reestablish community. "To walk in 'the way' as 'a people of the way' involves a moral style so intimately related to the destination itself that to wander from the way is also to miss the goal, which is a righteous life in a community faithful to God. . . ."[15] No one would suggest that the Book of Common Prayer is *the* answer to a disciplined way, but it is one answer that has a long history of use and a careful history of development.

These elements of a vocation do not of course exhaust the vocation of the Anglican Communion. What emerges from them is the picture of Christian communities drawn together by the bonds they have with the One who calls us always beyond the limited vision of our bonding. I am convinced that this vision to a vocation in fact matches much of what we as Anglicans are really like in our better moments. When all the hand-wringing about Anglican identity, theology, and ecclesiology is over and done with, when all the internal nervousness about having a future is expressed, when all our senses of superiority and inferiority are finally out in the open, we are mostly what has been expressed here.

The Anglican Communion sets the gospel, not itself, first; it sees itself as provisional, a fellowship within the whole church committed to the restoration of unity, a community of mutuality, a community of common prayer.

Considering this sort of reading of our present and future vocation, what might some of the practical consequences be for the Anglican Communion? The reader can produce a list. Here is my own:

• A commitment to the gospel rather than the church should lead the Anglican Communion through its visible leaders, communications and deliberations, to worry less about issues of growth of the Anglican Communion and its churches, and to a greater concern for shaping and informing local *koinonia,* communities of faith and "moral conviction," so that their faith and conviction reflect locally the experience of the whole Christian community.

• The meetings of primates, the bishops at Lambeth, and the ACC should primarily concern issues of encouragement and interconnection of local communities, and less often efforts to make declarations or definitive judgments about their actions.

Careful thinking and deliberate action by Anglican Communion bodies can lend weight to social and political change, and are to that end both prophetic and very helpful. But what the people of the Way need is primarily encouragement. With encouragement they will force the issues of greatest importance to them and bring them to the widest bodies of Anglican deliberation. The practical implication of the centrality of the gospel vis-à-vis social and political decision-making is that, from the standpoint of the gospel, the "kingdom of nuisances and nobodies"[16] will reign.

• The Archbishop of Canterbury has a primary role in this work of encouragement, as do the Primates. When they travel they are a symbol of the caring the wider Anglican community has for the struggles in place.

• There is a great temptation to see the Anglican Communion as a world church and to expect it to have all the characteristics of such a church. The great models for this are the patriarchates of Rome and Constantinople. But their actions make it clear that neither consider themselves in any way provisional. So the practical implication of the stance of provisionality is to avoid the temptation to be as others are.

While this has some implications for the role we give the Archbishop of Canterbury, it has even greater implications for the role assigned the Secretary General of the Anglican Consultative Council. The Secretary General will be greatly tempted to be able to speak on behalf of the communion or the Archbishop of Canterbury in authoritative ways. When asked, "What do Anglicans believe?" he or she will be sometimes embarrassed among peers to have to say, "It is unclear," or "We believe a variety of things on this matter," or worse yet, "There is no distinctively Anglican doctrine." It will be a great temptation to return from such peer meetings and make a strong plea for greater doctrinal and institutional clarity. The implication of the primacy in our vocation of the gospel and of our provisional stance is simple: do not give in to the temptation to solidify Anglican doctrine or the role of its leadership on models that we need not follow.

• A practical requirement for fellowship and mutuality is open communication, communication that is marked by transparency, trust and accountability. The communion will need to expand its networking on many levels—exchanges of personnel, consultations and conferences, sharing of ideas on the practice of faith in the world.

Communication is quite often a buzzword whose underlying organizational meaning is *communication for control*. We may communicate our needs, but the organizations and leaders tend to control our access to the means of meeting those needs. We are heard, but we have no control over what is done with what is heard. However, communication can also be about "mutual" engagement, the exchange of ideas, feelings, beliefs, etc., for the benefit of the communicators in their ministries in the world. If it is to be *communication for exchange and change* rather than control, certain tools are better than others. One of the most interesting is of course the free-for-all called the Internet.

The explorations into this medium have already started. It is possible from many places in the world to send electronic mail to the Archbishop of Canterbury. The question is, why would we do so? It only makes sense to do so if it could in fact make a difference—if there really was an exchange that could contribute to change. It is also possible to send electronic mail to someone by way of an open meeting, so that others participate in the communication. Increasingly the Internet opens up a means of sharing beyond the limits of our own location or communion. There is an almost built-in ecumenical component to electronic communication—it lends itself to a kind of openness not unlike the sharing of information throughout Europe following the invention of the printing press. The practical implication of this for a vocation to mutuality, restoration to unity, and fellowship is that we must work to make such communications an occasion for renewed transparency, honesty, and openness.

Anglican Communion meetings will need to practice an openness of theological exchange in the face of mounting calls for a new orthodoxy. For Anglican theological work, the implications of provisionality and the need for transparency in communication are clear: techniques of mutual criticism need to be developed in which Anglican method is encouraged rather than the demand for orthodox conclusions.

For the last eight years there has been an effort by the ACC to produce a "Common Declaration" that would clearly state the self-understanding of Anglican churches. That effort will continue in one form or another, but needs to be watched carefully at a time of renewed pressure for identity and orthodoxy.

The declaration has had a difficult history, and it is not clear where it will ultimately happen to it. One can only hope that it will not be used as a supplemental creed, or loyalty oath. Its content parallels the concerns of the Lambeth Quadrilateral and such statements as that of the preamble to the constitution of the Episcopal Church. Its fourth point is at the core of the specifically "Anglican" charter of this declaration.

> It [the Church of the Province of. . .] expresses its continuity with the apostolic tradition of faith and witness, worship, fellowship and ministry by means of the historic Episcopal order. It is in communion with each of those Churches which preserve the historic threefold order of the ordained ministry and are in communion with the See of Canterbury."[17]

The problem with this section of the declaration is that it defines the Anglican Communion "by means" of its ordained ministry, the historic episcopate, and the See of Canterbury. This definition seems a top-down one. Certainly, the ministry and the See of Canterbury may be instruments by which communion is described. But if this is the fellowship within the one, holy, catholic, and apostolic church that is primary, it is not about bishops but about people. The connections may be by way of bishops, but the declaration does not describe the primacy of the fellowship where it is most strongly present—as a local fellowship of people on the Way. What is needed is a common declaration that is indeed inclusive of the ministry of all its members.

There is every reason to wish for some way of identifying ourselves, in terms of a common declaration. However this one falls back into the problem of the means and the end. Bishops, and the identification by communion with Canterbury, are means to an end—the end being a fellowship with a common ordering of life and prayer. The declaration seems more limited than the Lambeth Quadrilateral, which affirmed, "The Historic Episcopate, locally adapted in the methods of its administration to the varying needs of the nations and peoples called of God into the Unity of His Church."[18] That at least acknowledges that it is the "needs of the peoples called of God" that determines what the episcopate will look like, not the historic roles as defined by the existing episcopal office in Anglican churches. There is more work to be done.

A VOCATIONAL MANIFESTO FOR THE ANGLICAN COMMUNION IN A POST-MODERN AGE

Here are six major vocational statements or goals drawn from or at least implied in what I have written. They are stated as a manifesto, as if they are manifest for all to see or have been made manifest in what has been written. I know that this is not the case. They remain partial and limited by virtue of my own partiality and limitations. But I believe they hold the seeds of a vocational direction for the Anglican Communion.

1. THE GOSPEL, NOT THE CHURCH, AS FIRST PRIORITY

The Anglican Communion and individual Anglican churches find a common cause in the gospel of Jesus Christ and live that out in shared practice. Our vocation is to place the gospel first, proclaiming it as well as possible and as we have lived and understand it in incarnational context, honoring the common life as we are able.

2. PROVISIONALITY

The Anglican Communion is a provisional conciliar body, and Anglicans are a provisional people. We retain this stance in our vocation, knowing, too, that even this stance has its own provisionality.

3. FELLOWSHIP

The Anglican Communion is a koinonia, *and Anglicans exist only in* koinonia—*in fellowship— rather than as a separate church. Our vocation is to insist that we are not the church, but only a fellowship within it, and to act on that belief.*

4. RESTORATION TO UNITY

The Anglican Communion lives conscious of the call to unity that lies beyond itself and all other communities of faith, and Anglicans pray for and identify with the catholic church. The vocation of the Anglican Communion is continually to live for that time when our separations dissolve in that obedience to Christ which is perfect freedom.

5. MUTUALITY

The Anglican Communion is a community rather than an organization, and Anglican churches are primarily identified as communities of prayer and mutual support in ministry. The Anglican Communion therefore has a vocation to community life—to mutuality, to shared authority, to different levels of engagement among its members—rather than to a set organizational structure.

6. COMMON PRAYER

The Anglican Communion has been informed and formed by the Book of Common Prayer, and Anglicans are identified with an ordered life of prayer and sacrament. The communion's vocation is to carry its liturgical and spiritual sense of common prayer into an ecumenical future, as one contribution to the building up of communities of the Way in an increasingly fragmented world.

These six together describe a fellowship very much identified with traditional Anglican marks and method, incarnational theology and experience. Yet in many ways these also describe a fellowship willing to die as well. In 1920, the Lambeth Conference reported the mind of the bishops at that time: "We aim. . .at extending not the Anglican Church with its special characteristics, but the Holy Catholic Church in its essentials, which each new Church, as it grows up, may exhibit under characteristics of its own."[19]

Anglicans express the courage, in many ways, to work for an end other than their own communion. It is perhaps our most wonderful legacy, for its basis is in humility. Regrettably, it is a virtue not often practiced by religious organizations in these days.

At the outset I indicated where I thought this book would take us: I suggested that the Anglican Communion should be supported and encouraged as a fellowship, a *koinonia*, rather than as an organization per se. To be effective, support and encouragement for this fellowship requires familiarity. That is what I have tried to do: to provide enough familiarity with some of the characteristics of this fellowship. I have argued that this fellowship is not easily described in organizational terms. There are no easily defined beliefs peculiar to Anglican churches, distinguishing them from all other Christian churches. The Anglican Communion's organizational assumptions are mostly at the episcopal level. Provincial organization and power varies throughout the communion. Communion-wide authority, power, and organization is real, but in actuality quite limited.

I have tried to indicate that our own provisionality and hope for restoration to unity precludes our becoming too set on organizational structure. Our attention is drawn elsewhere, and from the viewpoint of faith, that is precisely what ought to be the case. We are drawn away from being a church and toward being a people on the Way, precisely insofar as we are drawn to the gospel. For it is in the gospel that we see Jesus as receiving and eating with a whole world of people who were outside the assembly self-defined by the people assembled.

Fellowship is always *potentially* wider than assembly. *Koinonia* is always potentially wider than *ekklesia*. We are called as the Anglican Communion to live with the tension that we do assemble—sometimes as bishops at Lambeth, sometimes as bishops, clergy, and laity in convocation or convention, sometimes in parish meeting and liturgy—but we do so knowing that those who come do not exhaust the lists of our sisters and brothers who should be and will be invited. When our identification is with the assembly it already limits the possibilities of the fellowship. The *only* assembly that can draw our allegiance is that of the Body of Christ, and that is known as a reality only in Christ's Body and in the assembly before God in the end-time. We are drawn therefore to the Incarnation, which is known in Jesus, known in creation and in community, and known at the end. Our call is to a ministry of mutuality and compassion, to reconciliation and restoration. Even this vocation is not particular to us. So our vocation is always larger than our limitations of church order and governance can provide.

There will be no enduring Anglican Communion, not if we can help it. But that is not the point. Being Anglican is simply the way some Christians have tried to work out the implications of baptism in specific times and locations. What we have been will be of value to those who come after, and they will count us as among their ancestors. In doing so we have been greatly blessed by God. Often we have been under judgment by God, and yet most often led by God to what it is we are called to next.

The vocation of the Anglican Communion is to be a force for greater *koinonia*, for overcoming the fragmentation of life in a vision of the whole people of God, in a time when fragmentation is what seems to be the rule of the day. It remains only for us to take heart in our "looking to Jesus the pioneer and perfecter of our faith, who for the sake of the joy that was set before him endured the cross" (Heb. 12:1b–2a).

ENDNOTES

1. Westcott, *Catholic Principles*, 15–16.

2. Kew and White, *New Millennium, New Church*, 97.

3. Ibid., 98.

4. Ibid., 97.

5. The Book of Common Prayer, 876.

6. Kew and White, ibid., 47.

7. It is something like this principle that is at the core of the proposed concordat between the Episcopal Church and the Evangelical Lutheran Church of America. This proposal was passed by the 1997 General Convention of the Episcopal Church and regrettably failed to pass in the Lutheran Assembly. It has been an instructive effort, if for no other reason than that it has reaffirmed this principle in the Episcopal Church.

8. A disturbing development has occurred in England with the institution of "flying bishops," those who will exercise episcopal office for people and parishes that do not accept women in ordained ministry. Every parish and every diocese will then find itself having to choose to align itself with one of two incarnational styles. The question is whether this approach embraces provisionality or pluralism. Provisionality does not mean that the community

holds several different and quite incompatible views, but rather that it holds what it does hold provisionally. Pluralism would allow for a variety of different religious expressions, each the honest expression of a particular community. One can live in a pluralistic environment and not be provisional at all.

9. The Book of Common Prayer 1549, in Harrison, ed., *The First and Second Prayer Books of Edward VI*, 3.

10. A difficult example of this is the current movement in the Roman Catholic Church to elevate Mary to being with Our Lord "Co-Redeemer." The hope by some is that the Pope will exercise his powers to make that doctrine binding on the church. That so much power might be vested in one individual belies any impression of mutuality.

11. As an example, in October 1996, the Archbishop of Canterbury and the ACC took lead roles in declaring that the bishops of four dioceses in Rwanda had vacated their sees, and that therefore new elections were required. The Archbishop and the ACC exercised authority, on behalf of these dioceses, in a way that would allow these churches to reform.

12. Rasmussen, *Moral Fragments and Moral Community*, 9.

13. Ibid.

14. Ibid., 138ff.

15. Ibid., 139.

16. John Dominic Crossan's happy phrase for what in our day is reflected in the notion of base communities. See Crossan, *Jesus: A Revolutionary Biography*, chap. 3.

17. *Anglicanism and the Universal Church*, 239.

18. The Book of Common Prayer, 877.

19. Avis, *Anglicanism and the Universal Church*, 177.

BIBLIOGRAPHY

Allchin, A. M. *Participation in God: A Forgotten Strand in Anglican Tradition.* Wilton, Conn.: Morehouse-Barlow Co., 1988.

Anderson, Donald. "An Anglican Vision for the World Council of Churches." *The Ecumenical Review* 46 (1994): 394–405.

Anglican Consultative Council. *The Time is Now: Anglican Consultative Council, First Meeting, Limuru, Kenya.* London: SPCK, 1971.

Anglican Consultative Council. *Inter-Anglican Theological and Doctrinal Commission: Belonging Together.* London: Anglican Consultative Council, 1993.

Armentrout, Donald S., ed. *This Sacred History: Anglican Reflections for John Booty.* Cambridge, Mass.: Cowley Publications, 1990.

Avis, Paul. *Anglicanism and the Christian Church.* Philadelphia: Fortress Press, 1989.

Baum, Gregory. *Compassion and Solidarity.* New York: Paulist Press, 1990.

Bayne, Stephen F., Jr. *An Anglican Turning Point.* Austin, Texas: Church Historical Society, 1964.

———, ed. *Mutual Responsibility and Interdependence in the Body of Christ.* New York: Seabury Press, 1963.

Berger, Peter L. *A Far Glory.* New York: Macmillan, 1992.

Bonhoeffer, Dietrich. *Christ the Center.* Trans. John Bowden. Intro. E. H. Robertson. New York: Harper & Row, 1966.

The Book of Common Prayer. New York: Church Hymnal Corporation, 1979.

The Book of Common Prayer 1662.

Booty, John. *The Christ We Know.* Cambridge, Mass.: Cowley Publications, 1987.

Borg, Marcus J. *Meeting Jesus Again for the First Time: The Historical Jesus and the Heart of Contemporary Faith.* New York: HarperCollins, 1994.

Bosch, David J. *Transforming Mission: Paradigm Shifts in Theology of Mission.* Maryknoll, N.Y.: Orbis Books, 1991.

Cone, James H. *A Black Theology of Liberation.* 2nd ed. Maryknoll, N.Y.: Orbis Books, 1986.

————. *God of the Oppressed*. San Francisco: Harper & Row, 1975.

Cox, Harvey. *Many Mansions*. 2nd ed. Boston: Beacon Press, 1992.

Crossan, John Dominic. *The Essential Jesus: Original Sayings and Earliest Images*. New York: HarperCollins, 1994.

————. *Jesus: A Revolutionary Biography*. New York: HarperCollins, 1994.

————. "The Life of a Mediterranean Jewish Peasant." *Christian Century* 108 (1991): 1195–1200.

Douglas, Ian T. *Fling Out the Banner: The National Church Ideal and the Foreign Mission of the Episcopal Church*. New York: Church Hymnal Corporation, 1996.

Eliot, Thomas Stearns. *Four Quartets*. New York: Harcourt, Brace & World, 1943.

Ellsberg, Robert, and Mohandas K. Gandhi. *Gandhi on Christianity*. Maryknoll, N.Y.: Orbis Books, 1991.

Episcopal Divinity School, Faculty of. *Response to Belonging Together*. Cambridge, Mass.: Episcopal Divinity School, 1993.

Fox, Matthew. A *Spirituality Named Compassion*. 2nd ed., with a new preface by the author. New York: HarperCollins, 1990; first published 1979.

General Convention of the Episcopal Church. *Annotated Constitution and Canons for the Government of the Protestant Epsicopal Church in the United States of America, otherwise known as The Episcopal Church*. 2 vols. New York: Church Publishing Incorporated, 1997.

Gore, Charles, ed. *Lux Mundi: A Series of Studies in the Religion of the Incarnation*. 13th ed. New York: Thomas Whittacker, 1890.

Harrison, Douglas, ed. *The First and Second Prayer Books of Edward VI*. London: Everyman's Library, 1968.

Heuss, John. *The Implications of the Toronto Manifesto*. Evanston, Ill.: Seabury-Western Theological Seminary, 1965.

Heyward, Carter, and Ellen C. Davis, eds. *Speaking of Christ: a Lesbian Feminist Voice*. New York: Pilgrim Press, 1989.

Heyward, Carter, and Sue Phillips. *No Easy Peace: Liberating Anglicanism*. Lanham, Md.: University Press of America, 1992.

Hick, John. *The Metaphor of God Incarnate: Christology in a Pluralist Age*. Louisville, Ky.: Westminster/John Knox Press, 1994.

————, ed. *The Myth of God Incarnate.* London: SCM Press, 1977.

Hill, Christopher. *The English Bible and the Seventeenth-Century Revolution.* New York: Penguin Books, 1993.

Hodgson, Peter C. *Revisioning the Church: Freedom in the New Paradigm.* Philadelphia: Fortress Press, 1988.

Holloway, Richard, ed. *The Anglican Tradition.* London: Mowbray, 1984.

Holmes, David L. *A Brief History of the Episcopal Church.* Valley Forge, Pa.: Trinity Press International, 1993.

Holmes, Urban T., III. *What is Anglicanism?* Wilton, Conn.: Morehouse-Barlow, 1982.

Hooker, Richard. *Laws of Ecclesiastical Polity. Works of Richard Hooker.* Cambridge, Mass.: Harvard University Press, 1976.

Howe, John. *Anglicanism & the Universal Church: Highways & Hedges 1958–1984.* Intro. Colin Craston. Toronto: Anglican Book Centre, 1990.

Irenaeus of Lyons. *The Scandal of the Incarnation: Irenaeus Against the Heresies.* Ed. Hans Urs von Balthasar. Trans. John Saward. San Francisco: Ignatius Press, 1990.

Junkin, Edward Dixon. "Up from the Grassroots: The Church in Transition." *Interpretation* 46 (1992): 271–80.

Kew, Richard, and Roger J.White. *New Millennium, New Church.* Cambridge, Mass.: Cowley Publications, 1992.

Kittel, Gerhard. *Theological Dictionary of the New Testament.* Trans. and ed. G. W. Bromiley. Grand Rapids, Mich.: Eerdmans, 1964. Vol. 3, s.v. koinonia.

Koenig, John. *New Testament Hospitality.* Philadelphia: Fortress Press, 1985.

Long, Charles H., ed. *Who are the Anglicans?* Cincinnati, Ohio: Forward Movement Publications, 1988.

Marshall, Michael E. *The Anglican Church Today and Tomorrow.* Wilton, Conn.: Morehouse-Barlow, 1984.

McFague, Sallie. *The Body of God: An Ecological Theology.* Minneapolis: Fortress Press, 1993.

McGeary, Laura, John Martin, and James Rosenthal, eds. *A Transforming Vision: Suffering and Glory in God's World.* London: Church House Publications, 1993.

McGrath, Alister. *The Renewal of Anglicanism.* London: SPCK, 1993.

Morgan, Dewi. *Agenda for Anglicans*. Intro. Stephen Bayne. New York: Morehouse-Barlow, 1963.

Neill, Stephen. *Anglicanism*. 3rd ed. Baltimore, Md.: Penguin Books, 1963. 4th ed. New York: Oxford University Press, 1977.

————. *A History of Christian Missions*. 2nd ed. New York: Penguin Books, 1986.

Ramsey, Michael. *The Anglican Spirit*. Ed. Dale Coleman. Cambridge, Mass.: Cowley Publications, 1991.

Rasmussen, Larry L. *Moral Fragments and Moral Community*. Minneapolis: Fortress Press, 1993.

Rawlinson, A. E. J. *The Anglican Communion in Christendom*. London: SPCK, 1960.

Robinson, John A. T. *Honest to God*. London: SCM Press, 1963.

————. *The Human Face of God*. London: SCM Press, 1973.

Rowell, Geoffrey, ed. *The English Religious Tradition and the Genius of Anglicanism*. Nashville, Tenn.: Abingdon Press, 1992.

Russell, Letty M. *The Church in the Round: Feminist Interpretation of the Church*. Louisville, Ky.: Westminster/John Knox Press, 1993.

Russell, Keith A. *In Search of the Church*. Washington, D.C.: Alban Institute, 1994.

Sachs, William L. *The Transformation of Anglicanism from State Church to Global Communion*. Cambridge: Cambridge University Press, 1993.

Song, C. S. *The Compassionate God*. Maryknoll, N.Y.: Orbis Books, 1982.

Stendahl, Krister. "From God's Perspective We Are All Minorities," *Journal of Religious Pluralism* 2 (1993): 1–13.

Stevenson, Kenneth, and Bryan Spinks, eds. *The Identity of Anglican Worship* (Harrisburg, Pa.: Morehouse Publishing, 1991).

Sykes, Stephen W. and John Booty, eds., *The Study of Anglicanism*, London, SPCK, 1988.

Sykes, Stephen W., *Authority in the Anglican Communion*, Toronto: Anglican Book Centre, 1987.

Sykes, Stephen, P. H. E.Thomas, and Neville W. de Souza. *Four Documents on Authority in the Anglican Communion*. London: Anglican Consultative Council, 1981.

Thompsett, Fredrica Harris. *Courageous Incarnation in Intimacy, Work, Childhood, and Aging*. Cambridge, Mass.: Cowley Publications, 1993.

————. *We Are Theologians*. Cambridge, Mass.: Cowley Publications, 1989.

————. *Anglicanism Present and Future*. Washington D.C., Washington Cathedral, 1992.

Tillich, Paul. *Theology of Culture*. New York: Oxford University Press, 1959.

————. *Systematic Theology*. 3 vols. Chicago: University of Chicago Press, 1951–1963.

Turner, Philip W., and Frank Sugeno, eds. *Crossroads Are for Meeting*. Sewanee, Tenn.: SPCK/USA, 1986.

Tutu, Desmond Mpilo. *Hope and Suffering: Sermons and Speeches*. Ed. Mothobi Mutloatse. Johannesburg: Skotaville Publishers, 1982.

————. *The Theologian and the Gospel of Freedom*, Johannesburg: Skotaville Publishers, 1986.

Webster, Douglas. *Mutual Irresponsibility: A Danger to Be Avoided*. London: SPCK, 1965.

Westcott, Frank. *Catholic Principles, as Illustrated in the Doctrine, History and Organization of the American Catholic Church in the United States, commonly called the Protestant Episcopal Church*. Milwaukee: Young Churchmen Co., 1902.

Whale, John. *The Anglican Church Today: The Future of Anglicanism*. London: Mowbray, 1988.

Wolf, William J., John E. Booty, and Owen C. Thomas. *The Spirit of Anglicanism: Hooker, Marurice, Temple*. Wilton, Conn.: Morehouse-Barlow, 1979.

Wright, J. Robert. *Quadrilateral at One Hundred*. Cincinnati, Ohio.: Forward Movement, 1988.

Young, Francis. *The Making of the Creeds*. Philadelphia: Trinity Press International, 1991.

ABOUT THE AUTHOR

Mark Harris is an Episcopal priest who served for twelve years on the national staff of the Episcopal Church, working first in higher education ministry and then in missionary engagement with churches throughout the Anglican Communion. He has been a missionary to Puerto Rico and a chaplain at the University of Michigan and the University of Delaware.

He was editor of *Plumbline: A Journal of Higher Education* and has edited a book on higher education ministry. He has also published a number of articles and poems. He received his Doctor of Ministry degree from the Episcopal Divinity School, Cambridge, Massachusetts, in 1995.

Mark Harris and his wife Kathryn live in Newark, Delaware, where he is rector of St. James Church. For eight years the Harrises lived in a community called Good Hope. They dream of living in community again.